ESSENTIAL ELEME
CAREER COUNSEL

PROCESSES AND TECHNIQUES

SECOND EDITION

Norman E. Amundson

University of British Columbia

JoAnn Harris-Bowlsbey

Kuder, Inc.

Spencer G. Niles

Pennsylvania State University

Merrill
is an imprint of

Upper Saddle River, New Jersey
Columbus, Ohio

Library of Congress Cataloging-in-Publication Data

Amundson, Norman E.
   Essential elements of career counseling : processes and techniques / Norman
  E. Amundson, JoAnn Harris-Bowlsbey, Spencer G. Niles. —2nd ed.
     p. cm.
   Includes bibliographical references and index.
   ISBN-13: 978-0-13-158218-7 (alk. paper)
   ISBN-10: 0-13-158218-6 (alk. paper)
   1. Career development—United States. 2. Vocational guidance—United States.
  3. Educational counseling—United States. 4. Career development. 5. Vocational guidance.
  6. Educational counseling. I. Harris-Bowlsbey, JoAnn. II. Niles, Spencer G. III. Title.

HF5382.5.U5A718 2009
331.702—dc22   2007052873

Vice President and Executive Publisher: Jeffery W. Johnston
Publisher: Kevin M. Davis
Editor: Meredith D. Fossel
Editorial Assistant: Maren Vigilante
Marketing Coordinator: Brian Mounts
Production Manager: Kathy Sleys
Creative Director: Jayne Conte
Cover Design: Ilze Lemesis
Cover Illustration/Photo: Getty Images/Digital Vision
Full-Service Project Management/Composition: Karpagam Jagadeesan/GGS Books Services
Printer/Binder: R.R. Donnelley & Sons, Inc.

Credits and acknowledgments borrowed from other sources and reproduced, with permission, in this textbook appear on appropriate page within text.

Pearson Education Ltd., London
Pearson Education Singapore, Pte. Ltd
Pearson Education, Canada, Inc.
Pearson Education–Japan
Pearson Education Australia PTY, Limited

Pearson Education North Asia, Ltd., Hong Kong
Pearson Educación de Mexico, S.A. de C.V.
Pearson Education Malaysia, Pte. Ltd
Pearson Education Upper Saddle River, New Jersey

Merrill
is an imprint of

10 9 8 7 6 5 4 3 2 1
ISBN-13: 978-0-13-158218-7
ISBN-10:   0-13-158218-6

Preface

Over the years we have had the opportunity to develop programs and teach career counseling in many different settings. These settings include the school system, colleges and universities, unemployment centers, and immigrant transition services. All of these contexts present opportunities and challenges. What we have observed is that whatever the context, certain basic processes seem to define good career counseling.

In addition to our work within the United States and Canada, we have offered career counselor training in international contexts in both Europe and Asia. While there certainly were some cultural variables to be considered, there were some basic career counseling processes that seemed to fit a variety of intercultural contexts.

Though Chapter 2 reviews some of the theories of career choice and development, the book focuses primarily on practice by describing some of the basic career counseling techniques and resources that can be used to support them. We present information and a structure that is robust and, as such, can be widely applied. We also address some emerging issues such as Web-based counseling. To make the book more readable, we use case studies throughout.

Chapter 1 sets the foundation for the book. We affirm our belief in quality career counseling and explore various myths and emerging trends. In this chapter, we define career counseling and outline the competencies that counselors need to pursue as part of their training agenda. As a supplement to this chapter we include the NCDA guidelines for competency standards and ethical guidelines as appendices at the back of the book.

A starting point in counselor training is usually a basic understanding of some career counseling theories. With this in mind, in Chapter 2 we briefly examine the work of John L. Holland, Donald E. Super, and John D. Krumboltz, as well as the narrative approach of Mark L. Savickas. For illustration purposes we begin with a case study and then look at how the counseling process would differ depending on one's theoretical position.

In Chapter 3 we make the case that career counseling is more than an individual activity. It is important to take account of both individual and contextual variables. Career planning must be imbedded within social and economic realities. Donald Super's Archway of Determinants is used as a graphic illustration of the relationship of these variables.

The first three chapters lay a foundation for the career counseling process. In Chapter 4 there is an emphasis on the importance of the counseling relationship and an exploration of various ways of facilitating the relationship. There also are suggestions for how to cope with client reluctance.

In Chapter 5 the focus is on different ways of elaborating a client's career concerns. Part of this process is to define client constraint statements and to specify a clear direction. One way to view client concerns is to use metaphors as a means of visualizing the problem.

Chapters 6 and 7 address the exploration process. In Chapter 6, special attention is given to different ways of self-exploration. Within this chapter are illustrations of different questioning methods, storytelling, metaphors and structured assessment techniques. Chapter 7 shifts the exploration process to more contextual and economic factors. There also is consideration of how each person has his or her own personal labor market.

The impact of the World Wide Web on counseling is considerable, and in Chapter 8 we focus specifically on ways in which the web can support career counseling practice. We discuss various websites for career assessment and information and also provide some guidelines for how to evaluate the quality of websites. In keeping with the process orientation of this book, we also explore ways of using the website in various counseling situations.

In Chapter 9 we continue with the issue of web-based counseling and focus more specifically on the creation of virtual career centers. We discuss the components of a virtual career center, how local information needs to be incorporated, and ways of organizing the center for maximum effectiveness. Examples of sites are also provided.

Chapters 10, 11, and 12 move the counseling process forward from exploration to consolidation, decision making, action planning, evaluation, and follow-through. This is the point where information is brought together, decisions are made, and action plans are constructed. While this represents a specific counseling phase, it also is a time when sensitivity is needed to provide extra support and to revise plans when little progress is being made. The counseling process is not linear, and there needs to be a place for constant evaluation and adjustment.

The closing chapter, Chapter 13, briefly discusses some of the adaptations that need to be made to incorporate career counseling into various settings. In particular, we examine the school setting, the university, and different community contexts.

We hope we have accomplished our goals with this book. Most of our students have appreciated our practical emphasis on career counseling process and on the use of the Internet as a career counseling tool. In preparing the book we tried to present the material in a manner that is interesting, straightforward, and accessible to a wide range of people. We look forward to receiving your feedback about the material that we have included.

ACKNOWLEDGMENTS

Over the years I have had the opportunity to work closely with a number of colleagues and with them to participate in some interesting projects that have stretched my learning and professional development. These people and experiences have contributed to many of the ideas contained in this book. As I think about colleagues, I particularly would like to acknowledge Bill Borgen, Marv Westwood, and

Rod McCormick from U.B.C.; Ed Herr and Spencer Niles from Penn State University; and Gray Poehnell from Ergon Communications. With respect to counselor preparation, I have benefited greatly from my association with the clinics that are part of the U.B.C. training program. I have also benefited from the counselor training projects initiated by the Canadian federal government and from my collaboration with the University of Umea in Sweden. These projects helped refine my skills and also gave me the opportunity to extend my training to national and international levels.

From a personal perspective, I have been blessed with supportive family and friends. My wife, Jeanette, is involved in pastoral counseling, and together we have discussed and developed many innovative counseling processes and techniques. I am particularly thankful for the love and friendship that we share.

Norm Amundson

It has been my pleasure to be involved in the field of career development for forty years. When I was a young director of guidance in a large high school west of Chicago, I and members of my counseling staff received funding to develop one of the first computer-based career guidance systems. Involvement in that project made it possible for me to meet Dr. Donald E. Super and Dr. David V. Tiedeman and to participate in small invitational conferences that were held in the late 1960s about the potential to use the computer to assist others with career planning. These two giants in the career development field served as my mentors, and their stamp on my career has been indelible.

Since those early days, I have developed many versions of *DISCOVER* (a computer-based career planning system); counseled students at the university level; written career planning curriculum for middle, high school, and college-level students; and trained counselors and career development facilitators through face-to-face teaching, software, and curriculum development. It is my hope that, through this book, I can share some of what I have learned with the next generation of career counselors. Though supposedly retired, I continue to work avidly in the field and combine my two loves: career development theory and technology.

JoAnn Harris-Bowlsbey

I am deeply grateful to my students (at the University of Virginia, University of British Columbia, and Penn State University) and my career counseling clients who have taught me so much about what is important in career counseling. Opportunities to work with students in many countries have broadened my perspective and provided important learning experiences regarding career counseling. My professional colleagues, Ed Herr, Norm Amundson, JoAnn Harris-Bowlsbey, Mark Pope, and Ed Colozzi have each provided guidance and inspiration for which I am also grateful. Finally, the support and love of my family (Kathy, Jennifer, and Jonathan) had been essential as I have sorted through my own career decisions and tried to grow as a partner, father, and counselor educator.

Spencer Niles

All three of us would like to thank those who reviewed all or parts of the book while it was in manuscript form and in its first edition: Tracy Baldo, University of Northern Colorado; Andrew V. Beale, Virginia Commonwealth University; Chris Brown, University of Missouri–Kansas City; M. Harry Daniels, The University of Florida; Malka Edelman, Hofstra University; Debra A. Pender, Northern Illinois University; Linda Shapiro, University of Louisville; Nancy Wallace, George Mason University; and Jane Webber, Monmouth University. Their insights and guidance have made this a much better book than it would have been without their constructive input.

Brief Contents

Contents

Note: Every effort has been made to provide accurate and current Internet information in this book. However, the Internet and information posted on it are constantly changing, so it is inevitable that some of the Internet addresses listed in this textbook will change.

Career Counseling: Myths, Realities, and Emerging Trends

- **What Is Career Counseling?**

- **Factors Contributing to Shifts in Career Counseling**

- **Seven Common Career Counseling Myths**

- **Defining Career Counseling**

- **Career Counseling Competencies**

Career counseling is a cornerstone of the counseling profession. The first counseling-related professional association founded in the United States was the National Vocational Guidance Association (now the National Career Development Association (NCDA)), which was established in 1913. Much of the legislative support, which provides funding for counselor training and counseling activities, relates to the goal of providing career guidance to high-school students (National Defense Education Act of 1958; Career Education Incentive Act of 1976; School to Work Opportunities Act of 1994). Career interventions are central to the roles that counselors play in the school and university settings. A factor that distinguishes counseling from other helping professions, such as clinical psychology and social work, is that training in career counseling is a core requirement in counselor training programs but clinical psychologists and social workers usually do not receive such training. Thus, counselors often function as career development experts and can take pride in their long history of serving the career development needs of their clients.

This book strives to honor that history. The primary goal is to communicate the richness, vitality, and importance of career counseling. Creative approaches to helping people move forward in their career development are described. The career counseling strategies presented should enhance the repertoire of resources that career counselors use to help clients resolve career concerns.

WHAT IS CAREER COUNSELING?

If you ask an average person to define career counseling, there is a good chance that he will describe an experience that involves taking tests that tell him what he should do for a living. He may recall taking an interest inventory or aptitude test sometime during his high-school years. The odds are that he will have a vague recollection of his experience and will react with little enthusiasm if you were to ask how useful these activities were to him. Often, people note that the assessments told them what they already knew or worse—that the assessment results indicated that they should enter an occupation in which they have little interest.

The career counseling model that drives this variety of career counseling experiences emerged at the start of the previous century and finds its genesis in the work of Frank Parsons (1909). Parsons discussed various techniques that he found useful in helping the adolescents with whom he worked, first at the Breadwinners' College at the Civic Service House, a settlement house in Boston, and then at the Vocational Bureau of Boston. Specifically, the "Parsonian approach" consists of three steps used to help someone make an occupational choice. These steps are as follows:

1. Develop a clear understanding of yourself, aptitudes, abilities, interests, resources, limitations, and other qualities.
2. Develop knowledge of the requirements and conditions of success, advantages and disadvantages, compensation, opportunities, and prospects in different lines of work.
3. Use "true reasoning" on the relations of these two groups of facts (Parsons, 1909).

Parsons developed his model against a backdrop of social (rapid urbanization, child labor, immigration), economic (the rise of industrialism and the growing division of labor), and scientific (the emergence of human and behavioral sciences) changes occurring in the United States in the early 1900s (Niles & Harris-Bowlsbey, 2005). Parsons' approach fit nicely with the dominant scientific thinking of the 20th century, which emphasized logical positivism and objective methodology. The Parsonian model encouraged practitioners to objectify interests, values, and abilities through the use of standardized assessments to help people identify where they fit within the occupational structure. It is also the model that guides the understanding that most people have of modern career counseling.

It is not surprising, then, that when asked to identify the typical career counseling client and her career concerns, many people describe an adolescent trying to make a decision about which college to attend or which college major to choose. It is true that career counseling often includes taking assessments to clarify educational and career plans, and most adolescents need career assistance of various kinds. However, we are now experiencing a redefinition of career counseling, both in terms of the nature of career counseling and the developmental levels of people who seek career counseling assistance. It is now common for career counselors to incorporate a variety of interventions into their work with clients. Although standardized tests continue to be viable options for providing clients with self-information, counselors now realize that such measures offer partial solutions to complex career development concerns. Moreover, many people avail themselves of career counseling services far beyond their adolescent and early adult years. Career counselors supplement the traditional approaches to career intervention with counseling-based strategies that actively engage clients in the career counseling process. Moreover, career counselors collaborate with their clients to construct career interventions that address each client's concerns and context.

FACTORS CONTRIBUTING TO SHIFTS IN CAREER COUNSELING

Historically, career counseling interventions have been shaped by contextual influences (e.g., social, political, and economic factors). For example, over the past 100 years, career counseling has been influenced by:

social reform interacting with the rise of the industrial revolution in the late 1800s; the cognizance of individual differences in the early 1900s; the classification of military personnel and issues of national defense in the second decade of the 1900s; rising concern about people with disabilities and the mentally ill in the 1920s; the economic exigencies and needs to match persons with available employment opportunities during the Great Depression of the 1930s; national defense in the 1940s and the 1950s; the democratization of education, civil rights, women's rights, and occupational opportunities in the Great Society programs of the 1960s; concerns for equity and special needs populations in a climate of economic austerity in the 1970s;

and the transformation from an industrial to an information-based global economy and from military to economic competition among nations in the 1980s and 1990s (Herr, 2001, p. 202).

The shift from a military to economic competition among nations and the shift to an information-based economy leave many adults experiencing tenuous employment security. Workers experience anxiety about the prospect of being laid off from work because record downsizing is occurring in the United States and in other countries. Feeling the pressure to remain valuable at work leads many to commit more time to employers, leaving less time for other activities. The initial predictions that technology would create a "leisure society" have now given way to reality. Rather than creating more leisure time, advances in technology have made it easier (and often necessary) to work more hours. Information flows at unprecedented rates, and many workers feel the pressure to keep up. Unfortunately, technology can change work, but it cannot change the fact that days occur in 24-hour cycles. Workers in the United States work longer hours and take less vacation than workers in most other countries. The average working U.S. citizen now works approximately 200 hours more per year to maintain the same standard of living experienced in the early 1970s (Levey & Levey, 1998).

Additional changes in work are evidenced by the fact that organizational hierarchies are flattening, resulting in fewer career ladders to climb. Contingent work forces are emerging to replace long-term employees. Computers are replacing workers and adults are forced to acknowledge that, although they have a job today, they may be unemployed tomorrow—regardless of how competent they are or how hard they work (Rifkin, 1995). Many workers struggle to navigate the choppy waters they encounter at work. As they attempt to smooth their career turbulence, they realize that old solutions for increasing job security (such as working harder) have little impact on new situations. These shifts have led some to suggest that "work has ended" and the "career has died" (Bridges, 1994; Rifkin, 1995).

Citizens of the U.S. are not the only workers to experience excessive work hours and anxiety related to job security. Being overworked is not restricted by national boundaries. Levey and Levey (1998) note that, in Japan, the second leading cause of death (after cancer) is referred to as *karoshi*, which is defined as "death from over-work." In Canada, a recent survey indicated that 25% of working Canadians do not feel they can take annual vacation, in part, out of fear that their workload will be overwhelming when they return. Overwork is also not gender biased. Many women "report a lack of time together with their family as their greatest family concern" (Levey & Levey, 1998, p. 231). In fact, many dual career parents experience conflict trying to find time to fulfill their work and family commitments.

Moreover, these shifts in work are causing workers to reconsider their definitions of "success." As career ladders disappear and hard work is no longer a key to career achievement, a "successful" career can no longer be defined as reaching the top of the ladder. Many workers who have sacrificed everything for their employers now question that level of commitment when their employers seem so willing to sacrifice them. Not surprisingly, many now seek success in life—not just in work. Because our life structures reflect our individual values and commitments, success must be defined in personal terms. For many, the degree to which they are able to find opportunities for expressing their personal values in multiple life roles (e.g., work, family, and community) is becoming the yardstick they use to measure their success. Put another way: Rather than living to work, many people are deciding that it makes more sense to work to live.

These are some of the career development challenges that clients bring with them when they enter career counseling. Emerging career concerns can create confusion for many people because they collide with the historic, common understanding of career counseling. Career counseling clients are not clear about what is appropriate material to discuss with their career counselors (Niles, Anderson, & Cover, 2000). They expect to be tested, but they often seek more. Their confusion is heightened because their personal experience does not always connect with the common understanding of the career counseling process. Niles and his colleagues found that when career counselors provide clients with the opportunity to discuss how their non work concerns connect (sometimes collide) with their work concerns, they embrace the opportunity to do so. Thus, there seems ample evidence suggesting that holistic approaches to career intervention address client career concerns in the 21st century.

SEVEN COMMON CAREER COUNSELING MYTHS

The confusion surrounding the career counseling process can be summarized in the following common career counseling myths:

1. Career counselors have at their disposal standardized assessments that can be used to tell people which occupation they should choose.
2. Work role decisions can be made in isolation from other life roles.
3. Career counseling does not address "personal" issues.
4. Career counselors do not need extensive counseling expertise to do their work competently.
5. Career counseling does not address the client's context and culture.
6. Career counseling is required only when a career decision must be made.
7. Career counseling ends when a career decision is made.

These myths play themselves out in various ways. As previously noted, many clients enter career counseling expecting to take a test that will tell them what they should do. Because there is no such test, career counselors often need to provide appropriate structuring to their clients, especially in terms of client expectations for career counseling. Clarifying what is reasonable to expect helps clients understand what is possible and what is not. Appropriate structuring in career counseling also involves helping clients understand that work decisions cannot be made in isolation from other life roles. Although this statement seems obvious (because life roles interact), it is not uncommon for clients to think that all they will discuss in career counseling is work. Such a career counseling process would create a false scenario. Work-related decisions influence how much discretionary time one has, one's lifestyle, the sort of people one interacts with during the course of the day, and many other important factors. Life is not lived in isolated, compartmentalized life role "silos." Thus, career counseling must reflect life—as people live it—to be beneficial to clients.

There are few things more personal than career choices. Again, this seems to be a statement of the obvious. Consider the quality of life one experiences when work situations go awry. Many people experience psychological, physical, financial, and interpersonal distress at such times. Conversely, when work situations are positive, the likelihood of experiencing positive mental and physical health increases (Herr, 1989).

Clearly, these factors indicate that career counseling is a complex activity that encompasses a full range of clients' life experiences. Career development issues are human development issues. Helping clients address their career concerns holistically requires an advanced level of counseling expertise. One area of expertise career counselors must possess is multicultural competence. Career counselors must possess the knowledge, skills, and awareness necessary to help clients from diverse backgrounds cope with their career concerns. Understanding how race, ethnicity, socioeconomic status, gender, sexual orientation, physical abilities, family constellations, geography, and other contextual variables influence a client's world view, the career options the client is willing/able to consider, and the career counseling relationship are essential for providing effective career counseling assistance.

Unfortunately, the history of career counseling does not reflect a strong commitment toward being sensitive to diversity in clients. Many of the standardized assessments used in career counseling lack cultural equivalence, appropriate norm groups, and linguistic equivalence (Fouad, 1993). Historically, members of diverse racial and ethnic groups have been "guided" into a narrow range of occupational options in areas such as domestic service, food service, and education (Aubrey, 1977). Rather than providing services that fit the client's context, career counselors attempted to fit their clients to a particular career counseling approach. Career counseling strategies emphasized individualistic and rational approaches to career decision-making. Such strategies ignore those who approach decisions from a collectivistic orientation and use a more intuitive style of decision making. If the career counseling experience was not effective, it was usually the client's "fault." Avoiding such "culturally encapsulated" (Wrenn, 1962) approaches is essential for effective career counseling.

To reduce the occurrence of acting in culturally encapsulated ways, career counselors must commit to engaging in ongoing activities that foster multicultural awareness, knowledge, and sensitivity. Beginning with a clear understanding of how one's own family and cultural context influences one's life role conceptualizations is a useful starting place. Considering the messages inherited from one's family of origin regarding what is required to be a competent worker, parent, citizen, partner, etc. helps career counselors clarify the lenses they apply to their life role behavior. Life role orientations often carry strongly held values that may be functional and appropriate for one person but not for another. Cultural immersion experiences are also vital to fostering multicultural sensitivity. Traveling to other countries provides an excellent window into the ways in which nationalistic priorities and orientations infiltrate career decisions and the availability of specific occupational opportunities.

It is also important for career counselors to understand that career concerns span the life course and continue beyond the point at which a choice has been implemented. Because human development is a life long activity, career choice and adjustments are continual processes (Super, 1990). Work-related concerns ebb and flow, requiring career counseling assistance as people take greater responsibility for career self-management. Coping with coworkers, supervisors, job demands, and occupational stress is just one of the few examples of career concerns that might not necessarily result in the need to identify new career options.

DEFINING CAREER COUNSELING

This book's definition of career counseling emphasizes a life span and holistic approach. Specifically, career counseling is defined as the process in which a counselor works collaboratively to help clients/students clarify, specify, implement, and adjust to work-related decisions. Career counseling addresses the interaction of work with other life roles.

The NCDA provides direction in terms of the activities in which career counselors typically engage. These include the following:

- collaboratively administering and interpreting formal and informal assessments to help clients clarify and specify relevant self-characteristics (such as values, interest, and abilities)
- encouraging experience-based exploratory activities (such as job shadowing, externships, and occupational information interviews)
- using career planning systems and occupational information systems to help individuals better understand the world of work
- providing opportunities for improving decision-making skills
- assisting in the development of individualized career plans
- teaching job-search strategies, interview skills, and assisting in resume development
- helping to resolve potential personal conflicts on the job, through practice in developing relevant interpersonal skills (e.g., assertiveness training)
- assisting in understanding the integration of work and other life roles
- providing support for persons experiencing job stress, job loss, and/or career transition (www.ncda.org)

CAREER COUNSELING COMPETENCIES

The NCDA has identified the essential competencies required for career counseling. These competencies include 11 content areas that are briefly defined by the NCDA:

- Career development theory: Theory base and knowledge considered essential for professionals engaging in career counseling and development.
- Individual and group counseling skills: Individual and group counseling competencies considered essential for effective career counseling.

- Individual/group assessment: Individual/group assessment skills considered essential for professionals engaging in career counseling.
- Information/resources: Information/resource base and knowledge essential for professionals engaging in career counseling.
- Program promotion, management, and implementation: Skills necessary to develop, plan, implement, and manage comprehensive career development programs in a variety of settings.
- Coaching, consultation, and performance improvement: Knowledge and skills considered essential for enabling individuals and organizations to effectively impact the career counseling and development process.
- Diverse populations: Knowledge and skills considered essential for providing career counseling and development processes to diverse populations.
- Supervision: Knowledge and skills considered essential for critically evaluating counselor performance, maintaining and improving professional skills, and seeking assistance for others (when needed) in career counseling.
- Ethical/legal issues: Information base and knowledge essential for the ethical and legal practice of career counseling.
- Research/evaluation: Knowledge and skills considered essential for understanding and conducting research and evaluation in career counseling and development.
- Technology: Knowledge and skills considered essential for using technology to assist individuals with career planning (www.ncda.org, 1997).

NCDA's Career Counseling Competencies represent content domains in which career counselors must be competent.

Professional competency statements provide guidance for the minimum competencies necessary to effectively perform a particular occupation or job within a particular field. Skills and knowledge are represented by designated competency areas, which have been developed by professional career counselors and counselor educators. Career Counseling Competency Statements can serve as a guide for career counseling training programs or as a checklist for people who want to acquire or enhance their career counseling skills. Toward this goal, we recommend that you review the NCDA's Career Counseling Competencies and Performance Indicators (Appendix A). As you review the competencies, rate yourself according to the degree to which you think you possess each competency (1 = weak, 2 = average, and 3 = strong). Then, you may find it useful to develop a plan for strengthening your competency level for those competencies you rated yourself at either level 1 or level 2. Although many of the competencies listed are addressed in this book, not all of them are. Thus, you may find it useful to meet with your professor, advisor, and/or supervisor to develop a plan of action for increasing your competencies.

The ethical standards of the American Counseling Association and NCDA require career development professionals to only perform activities for which they "possess or have access to the necessary skills and resources for giving the kind of help that is needed." If a professional does not have the appropriate training or resources for the type of career concern presented, an appropriate referral must be made. No person should attempt to use skills (within these competency statements) for which she has not been trained. For additional ethical guidelines, refer to the NCDA Ethical Standards for Career Counselors in Appendix B.

Essential elements of effective career counseling include training that includes exposure to career interventions, being able to translate career counseling theory to practice, possessing multicultural competencies, and having knowledge and awareness of ethical standards. The following chapters present strategies for expanding your career counseling repertoire. The skills and knowledge mentioned above are emphasized, along with the importance of being able to integrate technology into the career counseling process. Key issues in establishing, developing, maintaining, and ending the career counseling process are addressed. Finally, some of the common career concerns that clients present in various counseling settings are highlighted. This book should be used as a resource that expands your working knowledge of career counseling. As a supplement to the information we provide in this book, we encourage you to become familiar with, and take advantage of, the resources provided by professional associations devoted to career interventions, such as the NCDA (www.ncda.org), the National Employment Counseling Association (NECA) (www.geocities.com/Athens/Acropolis/6491/neca.html), and the International Association for Educational and Vocational Guidance (IAEVG) (www.iaevg.org).

Using Career Theories to Help Clients

- **Theory of John L. Holland**

- **Theory of Donald E. Super**

- **The Narrative Approach of Mark L. Savickas**

- **Theory of John D. Krumboltz**

Sue, a sophomore at a state university, decided to go to college at the age of 27 after working at a sequence of unsatisfying jobs for the nine years since she graduated from high school. She inherited a small amount from an aunt, which has allowed her to reduce her work to half time at her job as a checkout clerk at a large grocery store. Sue is single, lives in a modest apartment in town, and commutes to the campus.

Sue is currently taking nine semester hours of college work, mostly graduation requirements, and holding a strong B average. By next semester, however, she needs to declare a major and begin to take courses in that field.

She initiates a visit to the counseling center on campus. On the intake form, she indicates that she needs to choose a major and get some idea about the kind of work she will do in the future. She is assigned to a counselor who specializes in assisting students who have career concerns.

One valuable reason for studying career development and choice theories is to provide a framework that counselors can use to guide their interventions with clients. The purpose of this chapter is to illustrate how counselors can use four different theoretical perspectives of career choice and development to deal with their clients. In order to accomplish that purpose, a case study is provided. Then, each of the theories is reviewed briefly and applied to the case. The goals, tools, and techniques that would be typical of each theoretical approach are reviewed, and typical counselor–client interaction is illustrated for the case.

The theoretical positions chosen for this chapter are those of John L. Holland, Donald E. Super, Mark L. Savickas, and John D. Krumboltz. Though there are other theoretical perspectives that offer valuable frameworks, tools, and techniques, it is impossible to attend to all of these within one chapter.

Though these theoretical perspectives are applicable to a wide range of clients and settings, it is also impossible, within this one chapter, to apply each to multiple cases. For that reason, the case study provided is that of a college student who has typical career needs and concerns. It is possible to use the same framework with clients and students of younger and older ages in a variety of settings, though the dialogue between the counselor and the client may need to be modified to attend to diversity of all kinds and to concerns that are unique for a given client, setting, or problem.

THEORY OF JOHN L. HOLLAND

Though Holland's theory gives some attention to heredity, the environment, and their influence on career choices, his emphasis is on the factors that impact choices at a given point in time. In other words, within his theoretical approach, a counselor would focus on the "now," rather than probe long-term career development prior to the time of the client's visit, or following the time of the next immediate choice point. With this case, however, the counselor will have interest in past work history because it is a strong indicator of present interests and skills.

Holland's theory can be summarized in four statements:

1. The personalities of individuals can be described as a combination of six types: realistic, investigative, artistic, social, enterprising, and conventional.
2. Environments (including occupations, specific jobs, programs of study, and leisure activities) can be described as a combination of the same six types.
3. Persons of a given type are attracted by environments of the same or a similar type.
4. Placing oneself in an environment of the same type, or one very similar to one's own, contributes significantly to the potential for an individual's satisfaction, persistence, and contribution in that environment.

Additional concepts that support practical application of these four statements include the following:

• The six types are clearly described in Holland's book, *Making Vocational Choices* (1997). Brief definitions of these types are as follows:

Realistic (R)
Likes to work with tools, objects, machines, or animals
Develops manual, mechanical, agricultural, and/or electrical skills
Prefers occupations that involve building or repairing things
Tends to be down to earth and practical

Investigative (I)
Likes activities involving the biological and physical sciences
Develops math and science ability
Prefers occupations in scientific and medical fields
Tends to be curious, studious, and independent

Artistic (A)
Likes creative activities free from routine
Develops skills in language, art, music, and drama
Prefers occupations using creative talents
Tends to be creative and free thinking

Social (S)
Likes activities that involve informing, teaching, and helping others
Develops ability to work with people
Prefers jobs such as teaching, nursing, and counseling
Tends to be helpful and friendly

Enterprising (E)
Likes activities that permit leading or influencing other people
Develops leadership ability, persuasiveness, and other important "people" skills

Prefers occupations involving sale of products or management of people
Tends to be ambitious, outgoing, energetic, and self-confident

Conventional (C)
Likes activities that permit organization of information in a clear and orderly way
Develops organizational, clerical, and arithmetical skills
Prefers occupations involving record-keeping, computation, typing, or computer operation
Tends to be responsible, dependable, and detail-oriented.

• An individual's type can be assessed in at least four ways: (1) administration of Holland's *Self-Directed Search* (Holland, 1994b) or *Vocational Preference Inventory* (Holland, 1985); (2) administration of instruments by other authors and publishers who use the Holland typology (perhaps with different names for the six types), including the *Kuder Career Search with Person Match*™ (Kuder & Zytowski, 2007), *Strong Interest Inventory* (Campbell, Strong, & Hansen, 1991), *Campbell Interest and Skill Survey* (Campbell, 1992), *O*Net Interest Profiler* (United States Employment Service, 2002), *Harrington-O'shea Career Decision-Making System* (Harrington & O'shea, 2000), and *Career Assessment Inventory* (Johansen, 1984); (3) informal assessment, including a structured interview, the Holland Party Game, or the Occupational Daydream section of the *Self-Directed Search*; or (4) analysis of past jobs held for which the client has interest and skills.

• The Holland code of a specific occupation can be measured by administering the *Self-Directed Search* or the *Vocational Preference Inventory* to a representative sample of individuals who indicate that they are satisfied in it, then calculating a mean code. Specific positions can be coded by administering the *Position Classification Inventory* (Gottfredson & Holland, 1996b) to those filling the position. Holland codes are provided for each occupation in the O*Net occupational database, the official online publication of the U.S. Department of Labor, available at http://online.onetcenter.org.

• The shape of an individual's profile on any of the instruments previously listed is an important piece of information. Profiles of the client's interests and self-perceived skills on the six types have differing levels of differentiation. *Differentiation* is defined as the numerical difference between the lowest and the highest scores for the six types. Profiles may be high and flat (high interest and perceived skill in all six areas), may be low and flat (low interest and perceived skill in all six areas), or may have peaks and valleys. Having at least one area of interest that is significantly higher than the rest is a positive condition, because it represents crystallization of interests in at least one area. This area, perhaps combined with one or two other areas in which there is also marked interest, provides an anchor point for exploration and generation of options. Persons who have high, flat profiles are likely to need assistance when choosing which two or three Holland groups to combine for work. Persons who have low, flat profiles may need assistance with exploration, because they do not appear to have crystallized interests at this time.

Consider these three different profiles and the meaning of each.

High, Flat Profile

```
50                            |
40            |       |       |       |       |       |
30            |       |       |       |       |       |
20            |       |       |       |       |       |
10            |       |       |       |       |       |
 0            |       |       |       |       |       |
              R       I       A       S       E       C
```

Meaning: The person whose raw scores on Holland's *Self-Directed Search* look like this has strong, and almost equal, interest in the work activities involved in all six Holland groups. In other words, this person is a multi-interested and perhaps also multitalented person. The counseling question becomes, then, which of these kinds of activities does the person want to do in paid employment (as no jobs would combine all six areas), and which does the person want to do in other life roles—such as citizen (i.e., volunteer work), leisure, and family (spouse and parent) roles? In making these choices, values may certainly come into play. The person may value both high income and helping others, for example. Unfortunately, most occupations that offer the potential to help others do not also provide high income. So, this person may choose to identify occupations coded with some combination of I and E because they have potential to provide high income. The client may choose to do S (helping others) activities in volunteer, citizen roles; and use A (Artistic), R (hands-on building and maintenance), and C (keeping things organized) interests in the roles of parent, homemaker, and spouse.

Well-differentiated Profile

```
50
40                                            |       |
30                                            |       |
20            |       |                       |       |
10            |       |       |       |       |
 0            |       |       |       |       |       |
              R       I       A       S       E       C
```

Meaning: Note that this person has high peaks in two areas—S and E—and average or low scores for the remaining four Holland types. This person, whether an adolescent or an adult, should be encouraged to consider majors (if still pursuing formal education or training) and occupations with the Holland codes SE or ES. Representative postsecondary majors would be Human Resources Management, Hospitality Marketing, and Real Estate; and representative occupations are employee benefits manager, employment interviewer, human resources manager, and training/education manager.

Low, Flat Profile

```
50
40
30
20            |            |
10            |     |     |     |     |     |
0             |     |     |     |     |     |
              R     I     A     S     E     C
```

Meaning: The most difficult of the three types of profiles to deal with is the low, flat profile. It may belong to an adolescent or college student who has had very little assistance with exploring the world of work, limited self-knowledge, and little or no work experience. Basically, this profile says that its owner has no significant areas of interests. If this profile belongs to a young person, the best response is to provide interventions designed to broaden knowledge about the world-of-work options and to deepen understanding of personal interests, skills, and values. Interventions may include use of computer-based systems and websites that foster broad exploration; group counseling or classroom instruction; informational interviewing; job shadowing; organized field trips and career days; and individual counseling. If this profile belongs to an adult, he or she may not have the luxury of exploration and retraining, making it necessary to choose a combination of two or more Holland types that are disliked less than others or in which some work experience has been gained. The person's level of education also comes into play here as well as the availability of jobs in the real world. For example, almost all occupations coded I (Investigative) in the first position require at least a bachelor's degree, while there are many occupations coded R (Realistic) and C (Conventional) that can be entered with a high school diploma and some on-the-job experience. Similarly, jobs in many occupations coded A (Artistic) in the first position may be scarce.

• There is a research-based relationship among the six Holland groups, resulting in the order of R, I, A, S, E, and C (starting at any point) on his famous hexagon,

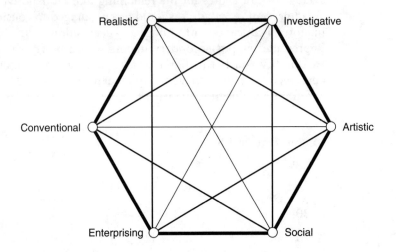

FIGURE 2.1 The Relationships among Holland Types

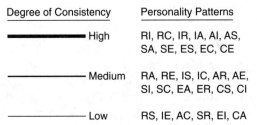

Degree of Consistency	Personality Patterns
━━━━━ High	RI, RC, IR, IA, AI, AS, SA, SE, ES, EC, CE
───── Medium	RA, RE, IS, IC, AR, AE, SI, SC, EA, ER, CS, CI
───── Low	RS, IE, AC, SR, EI, CA

Adapted from Holland's Hexagon, ACT Research Report No. 29, *by J. L. Holland, D.R. Whitney, N.S. Cole, and J.M. Richards, Jr., 1969, Iowa City: The American College Testing Program. Copyright © 1969 The American College Testing Program. Reprinted by permission.*

shown as Figure 2.1. This concept is called *consistency*. Individuals may have highly consistent codes (first two letters in the personal code are adjacent on the hexagon), moderately consistent codes (first two letters in the personal code are one point away from each other on the hexagon), or inconsistent codes (first two letters are opposite to each other on the hexagon). The code's degree of consistency provides some information about the similarity or dissimilarity (in terms of daily work tasks of a job) of a client's interests and about the potential to combine the client's interests in one job.

Consider the following combinations of codes that a person might have as you look at the hexagon in Figure 2.1.

- RI (and all others where the two environments are next door to each other)—a highly consistent code because the two letters are adjacent on the hexagon. This means that there may be many occupations (and jobs) that combine these two kinds of activities and that the person's two primary areas of interest are very compatible, requiring similar skills and offering somewhat similar environments.
- RA (and all others where the two environments are one point away from each other on the hexagon)—a code of moderate consistency because the two letters are one point apart on the hexagon. It may be more difficult, though not impossible, to find occupations (and jobs) that combine these two areas though they represent quite different environments.
- RS (and all other combinations that are across from each other on the hexagon)—a code of high inconsistency because the two environments are opposite from each other on the hexagon. In other words, the person's two highest areas of interest require very different kinds of skills and activities. In this case, the R environment requires the ability to work with one's hands, enjoying working alone, and getting satisfaction from seeing a tangible product completed. The S environment requires the ability to work face to face with people with good social skills, enjoying working closely with people to help them in some way, and getting satisfaction from doing so. Clearly, it is more difficult to find occupations (and jobs) that merge these opposites, and in some cases, individuals with such opposite codes have to choose one or the other environment rather than being able to merge both. Holland says that such opposite codes are formed because two very different streams of activities are positively reinforced in childhood, perhaps one area of interest by one parent and the other by the other parent.

COUNSELING GOALS

Within Holland's theory, the counselor's primary goals are as follows:

- Determine the client's present code and its characteristics (differentiation and consistency) in one of the ways previously listed.
- Using *The Educational Opportunities Finder* (Rosen, Holmberg, & Holland, 1999), find programs of study that match or are highly similar to the client's code, if choices about education or training are relevant.
- Using the *Occupations Finder* (Holland, 1994a), the *Dictionary of Holland Occupational Titles* (Gottfredson & Holland, 1996), or the O*Net database (U.S. Department of Labor, 2007), find occupations or jobs that match or are highly similar to the client's code—if choice of occupation, choice of jobs, or change in jobs is relevant.
- Using the *Leisure Activities Finder* (Holmberg, Rosen, & Holland, 1999), find leisure activities that match or are highly similar to the client's code, if use of personal time is an issue.
- Assist the client to gain information about the identified options.

For these reasons, the Holland approach is most appropriate for the following kinds of clients:

- those whose career concerns appear to be limited to identifying a major, an occupation, a job, or leisure activities
- those who do not appear to have barriers to exploration and decision making, such as irrational beliefs, poor self-efficacy, poor self-concept, or ineffective decision-making styles
- those who are in need of assistance at specific choice points (such as needing to declare a major, get a new job, or choose an occupation), but not long-term, developmental work.

SAMPLE COUNSELOR–CLIENT INTERCHANGE

Counselor	Hi, Sue. Please tell me why you came in today.
Sue	I'm in my sophomore year . . . came to college to get enough education to get a better job. So far I've been taking the required courses, but I need to declare a major by next semester.
Counselor	Which majors are you thinking about?
Sue	I don't have any idea . . . I just know that I'm tired of the boring jobs I've had to this point in my life.
Counselor	Any idea about the kinds of jobs you would like to have that would be more satisfying than jobs you have had?
Sue	No . . . I just know that I don't want to spend my whole life doing boring things and not getting paid much for it.
Counselor	What kinds of jobs have you had?
Sue	Receptionist, waitress, toll-booth collector, meter reader, and now grocery store clerk.
Counselor	Have there been any parts of those jobs that you have enjoyed?
Sue	I've enjoyed being able to talk to people in the receptionist, waitress, and grocery store jobs.

(The counselor continues this line of questioning about past jobs, school courses, and other activities to find activities that the client liked and disliked and begins to make some conclusions about which Holland types best describe this person. At the end of this first session, the counselor gives the client a copy of the Self-Directed Search *or the O*Net Interest Profiler and suggests that the client take it as one way of learning more about herself and identifying some majors and occupations. Another session is scheduled.)*

SECOND INTERVIEW

During the second interview, more progress is made.

Counselor	Last week I gave you a copy of an inventory called the *Self-Directed Search*. It's one way to learn more about your

	interests and skills. We can use its results to find some options—majors and occupations—for you to consider. Did you have a chance to complete it?
Sue	Yes, I did take it—very interesting. I went all the way through it and came up with my code.
Counselor	What was your code?
Sue	SER. The E was almost as high as the S, and R was a close third. I made a graph of my scores on this worksheet that you gave me (shows counselor a profile of the raw scores, showing S at 48, E at 46, R at 40, and the other three letters below 20).
Counselor	Do you know what that code means?
Sue	Yes, from reading the booklet that you gave me, I know that SER means that I like to work with people in some face-to-face way. The S says that I might like to help them in some way; the E says that I might like to sell them something or influence them, and the R means that I like to work with my hands. I've done a lot of that in some of my past jobs. I also used to help my dad a lot around the house.
Counselor	How do you react to this code as a description of your personality and interests?
Sue	It didn't surprise me at all. I told you last week that I have really enjoyed the parts of my jobs that allowed me to meet and talk with people. I was a little surprised by the R. I guess I'd never thought of my interest in that kind of stuff being applied to my next job.
Counselor	Because you do have some areas of interest that are considerably higher than the others, and your top two interests—S and E—are quite compatible, I think that you may be ready to look at some possible occupations and majors and begin to learn about them.
Sue	I already used the *Occupations Finder* you gave me, and I looked at the occupations with codes of SER.
Counselor	Did you see some that interested you?
Sue	Yes: health care facility administrator and orientation therapist for the blind. I didn't realize that I could do any high-level jobs related to health care without more than a college degree.
Counselor	Did you look at occupations coded ESR, because the E was almost as high as the S? That would pick up occupations such as manager of many different kinds of activities (points out the whole list on page 12), vocational rehabilitation consultant, and real-estate agent.
Sue	But what about my major?
Counselor	Let's try to focus in on some possible occupations first; then we can begin to relate majors to them. I see that you have

been making a list of occupations that appeal to you at first glance. Are you ready to learn about those in detail?

Sue   Yes, I think I am.

Counselor   Then let me give you a list of websites that have very detailed information about the occupations on your list. Read everything you can find about each of those occupations, and we'll discuss your findings in our next interview. We can also look in the *Educational Opportunities Finder* next time, begin to make a list of majors, and see which are offered here at the university.

THEORY OF DONALD E. SUPER

The contributions and theory of Donald E. Super are so far-reaching that condensing them and their application into a few pages is daunting. His work is concerned with both the length and the breadth of career development. His research identifies sequential life stages and developmental tasks relevant to career development, spanning from birth to death. His constructs include the Life-Career Rainbow, which includes activities in all interacting life roles as part of his definition of *career*. The breadth and depth of one's personal career is integrated by the continually emerging self-concept; and career choices are constantly mediated by that self-concept, other internal variables (such as values, interests, and abilities), and external variables (such as employment practices, job market, and economic conditions).

Despite the challenge of doing so, the most critical parts of Super's theory can be summarized as follows:

- One's career is influenced and mediated by one's self-concept, which begins its formation at the moment a baby can distinguish between self and other objects and people and continues to develop throughout the entire life span. Selection of an occupation is an implementation of one's self-concept (Super, 1963). One's self-concept can have many different characteristics—such as clarity, realism, self-regard, and detail. One of the primary roles of counselors is to assist clients to develop a strong, clear, and realistic self-concept, which includes an understanding of their interests, abilities, and values.
- Career development is a lifelong process that can be viewed in five distinct life stages: growth, exploration, establishment, maintenance, and disengagement. In the past, progression through these stages has been relatively linear. In the 21st century, however, many are experiencing iterative cycles of exploration, establishment, and maintenance, as an increasing portion of the population either chooses or is forced to work for different

employers and in different occupations rather than for one employer and in one occupation across the life span.

- As with many other skills, the skill of making effective career choices depends upon the possession of some specific kinds of knowledge (about decision making, self, the world of work, and specific occupations) and completing appropriate tasks (such as exploration and crystallization of options) at appropriate times. If this preliminary knowledge and these relevant skills have not been gained at appropriate age levels, there will be a later impact on career maturity, that is, the ability to cope well with career development tasks at a later life stage.
- The definition of *career* is far more than that of *job*. *Career* is a combination of all of the activities that take place in life roles being played by an individual at a given point in time (Super, 1980). These roles may include child, student, worker, spouse, parent, homemaker, citizen, and leisurite. They were depicted by Super as a Career Rainbow (see Figure 2.2). On the Career Rainbow, each role can be defined as the time and energy spent in the pursuit of that role. These roles interact with and affect each other. For example, the role of Worker is affected when a child is ill and the parent has to spend less or no time at work. Together they fill the life space, which is the

FIGURE 2.2 The Life-Career Rainbow: Six life roles in schematic life space. From *Career Choice and Development* (2nd ed.) , Duane Brown, Linda Brooks, and Associates

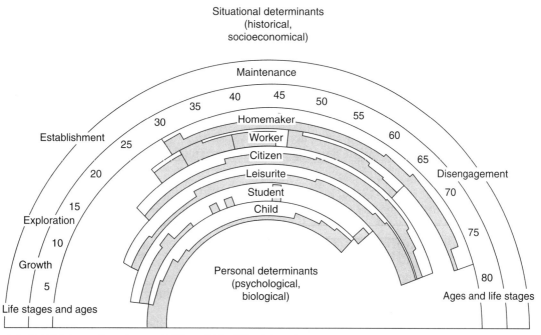

time that we each have in a day and in a lifetime. In Super's terms, successful career development is highly related to the ability to select life roles, manage their time (bandwidth) and importance (intensity), and live out one's self-concept and values through the blend of these roles.

- Notice that the earliest role is that of child followed by that of student and leisurite (the time and energy spent in recreational activities). The worker role is a very important one that influences and is influenced by all the other roles. During adult years, the roles of worker, spouse, homemaker, spouse, and citizen may all be played intensely. In general, Super concluded that the more roles an individual could play with appropriate balance, the higher the probability of life satisfaction and fulfillment. Role selection, bandwidth (time required), and intensity (importance) change over the life span, as some roles get less time consuming and intense (such as parent and worker) and others become more important (such as citizen or leisurite).
- Though the individual's self-concept, interests, values, abilities, and goals are prime factors in career choice and development, the conditions of the environment in which career choices are made are also strong influencers.

As with Holland, there are additional concepts related to Super's theory that have strong practical application:

- Some very important attitudes and skills need to be learned in early childhood in order to facilitate optimal career development. These include awareness of the need to plan ahead, decision-making skills, internal locus of control, and an attitude of exploration. Absence of these contributes to career immaturity.
- Values are very important influencers of career choice and development. Good knowledge of one's personal values assists in defining possible occupations. Values may, however, be distributed over life roles; one should not expect to attain all of one's important values in the worker role.

COUNSELING GOALS

In a Super frame of reference, the goals of career counseling are quite different from those cited for Holland's theoretical perspective. They would include any or all of the following:

- identifying the level of career maturity and attempting to reduce deficits found in possession of needed attitudes, skills, knowledge, and accomplishment of career development tasks
- analysis of self-concept and strengthening it through assessment and counseling, if appropriate
- understanding that a career is a combination of interacting life roles and assistance with selecting those roles and defining their dimensions in order to achieve balance in life
- identifying interests, abilities, and values and distributing them across life roles.

SAMPLE CLIENT–COUNSELOR INTERCHANGE

(The counselor has asked the career technician to administer the Adult Career Concerns Inventory *and the* Career Development Inventory *to the client prior to the first interview. Counselor has scores.)*

Counselor	Hi, Sue! Please begin by telling me why you made an appointment with me.
Sue	I'm in my sophomore year . . . came to college to get enough education to get a better job. So far I've been taking the required courses, but I need to declare a major by next semester.
Counselor	So, it's time to really think about who you are and what you want your life to be like.
Sue	I never thought of it that way—I was just thinking about which major to choose.
Counselor	That's really important . . . but it's just one step in a process. Do you have one or more occupations in mind that you would like to pursue?
Sue	No, I haven't really thought about that yet. I know that I'd like to work with people in some way, and I also seem to have ability with mechanical things.
Counselor	That's a start. Tell me the kinds of experiences you have had when working with people.
Sue	As a receptionist and grocery store clerk, I learned that I can communicate with people well and that I am willing to go beyond what my job requires in order to help them with a question or a problem. I get a lot of satisfaction from that.
Counselor	So, you see yourself as a person who has ability to help other people, and that is important to you.
Sue	Yes.
Counselor	Have you identified some occupations that would allow you to help others or work with others in ways that seem important to you?
Sue	Not really. I know that nurses help other people, but I don't think I want to work with sick people. I guess teachers help kids, but that doesn't appeal to me either.
Counselor	*(Scanning scores on the* CDI, *but not interpreting them to client.)* I think that a good next step would be for you to spend some time finding as many occupations as you can that would allow you to work with people. We have DISCOVER here— that's a computer-based career planning system. If you would use these two parts of DISCOVER (handing the client a marked flowchart of the system), I think that you would come up with a lot of possibilities. Print out the list of occupations you find; read their descriptions, and print those out, too. The next time you come, we'll discuss that list together.

SECOND INTERVIEW

After the client (Sue) does what the counselor asks, they meet to discuss her findings.

Counselor	So, did you come up with a lot of ideas? I guess you did—judging from the stack of printouts you have!
Sue	I found a lot of occupations in sales and management where I could work with people, and also a lot in health and human services and education. I found out that I could enter good jobs in any of those areas with a college degree, but there's quite a lot of difference in the majors that would lead to those different groups.
Counselor	Yes, that's correct. Tell me a little about how you want your life to be five, or even ten, years from now. Think about parts of your life other than work—such as whether you want to be married, have children, be active in the community, have time for leisure, or own your own home.
Sue	I've always dreamed of being married—and I'm dating someone steadily now—and of having at least two children. I want to be able to have my own home—enough of apartment living—and to have a good amount of time for family and community activities besides holding a full-time job.
Counselor	Sounds like a full and satisfying life! I'd like you to take three things home with you. If you will complete them, we will discuss them in detail in our next session. The first is this graphic of what I call the Life-Career Rainbow. It depicts the typical life roles that people play—the way they use their time and energy. I'd like you to use this worksheet to draw your own personal Career Rainbow—indicating which roles you'd like to play and how much of your time per week you'd like to spend in each. The second is called the Values Scale. It is an inventory that will help you to determine which of 21 values are most important for you. And finally, on this third worksheet, try to decide which of the values that you rate "most important" you want to use in each of the life roles you have chosen. Doing these activities will give you some information to use in reviewing each of the occupations you are considering for the worker role of your life. Hang in there! We'll get to your choice of major one of these days!

THE NARRATIVE APPROACH OF MARK L. SAVICKAS

Constructivist theory, represented by Savickas' narrative approach, is a 21st-century extension of Super's theory. You may recall that one central concept of Super's theory was his statement that "the choice of an occupation is the implementation of a self-concept." Defined by Savickas, a student of Super, constructivist theory proposes that individuals can create a career and give it meaning. This approach minimizes the 20th-century perspective that the traits of human beings can be measured and that jobs can then be found matching these traits. Advocates of the constructivist position underscore the fact that both individuals and environments change too rapidly in the 21st century to provide a match that has stability. In this theory, "careers do not unfold, they are constructed as individuals make choices that express their self-concepts and substantiate their goals in the social reality of life." (Savickas, 2005).

Conceptually, the theory includes three components: vocational personality, life themes, and career adaptability. The theory embraces the idea of differential psychology that each individual has a set of traits and that these traits constitute personality types (Holland, 1997) that can be matched to the characteristics of occupations. Constructivism views that match in a much more subjective way than does Holland, however, emphasizing *why* individuals engage in this type of vocational behavior and how it expresses a life theme.

The second component of the theory is life themes. The theoretical position proposes that the unique experiences that each individual has create one or more life themes. These themes may represent a problem that needs to be solved or a value that needs to be attained. The theme is, as expressed by Super, a driving force to express one's self-concept and to give meaning to work and other life roles. So, a central role of a counselor is to assist individuals to identify life themes and then to create ways to play out these themes in work, giving it deeper personal meaning and also making a contribution to society.

The third component of the theory is career adaptability. The rapid and complex changes of the 21st century demand flexibility and adaptability. Adaptability consists of the attitudes, behaviors, and competencies that individuals use in order to make the adjustments needed in their work environment or their career changes. Possession of these characteristics enhances the processes of altering the environment and adapting the self to be able to implement the self-concept in work.

The method used to assist individuals within this theoretical frame of reference is storytelling. That is, the counselor triggers life stories by asking the client some leading questions. The counselor's role is to identify themes that come from these life stories and to assist the client to recognize the themes. Once the themes are recognized, the selection of an occupation becomes the means of playing out the theme. Theoretically, being able to play out a deep-seated life theme through work significantly increases the meaning of that life role.

Typical questions that can be used by a counselor who is working within this theoretical perspective include the following:

- Can you tell me three of your earliest memories?
- Who were some of your most important role models, and why?
- What is your favorite movie (novel, magazine, TV show, etc.) and why?

It is believed that those stories that clients tell as a result of being triggered by questions such as these are the stories that embody significant life themes.

COUNSELING GOALS

1. To make the client aware of significant life themes and unresolved problems.
2. To help the client construct a career that will facilitate the use of this life theme or help solve this unresolved problem.
3. To help the client develop career adaptability in order to be able to cope with the ever-changing ways to implement self-concept in work.

SAMPLE CLIENT–COUNSELOR INTERCHANGE

Counselor	Thank you for coming in. How can I help you to construct your own career today?
Sue	I will soon have to declare a major, and I have no idea what I want to do when I grow up.
Counselor	So, you'd like us to focus on some possible occupational goals so that you could select a major that would support those goals.
Sue	Yes, that's right.
Counselor	Help me to learn more about you. Who were some of your earliest role models?
Sue	They were rock stars, like David Bowie . . . and adventurers like Jacques Cousteau
Counselor	And, what did you admire about them?
Sue	The freedom they seem to have. They can express themselves freely, wear anything they want to, or say anything they want to . . . and people still love them.
Counselor	So, not being hemmed in by tradition or artificial restraints appeals to you. What else can you tell me about you? As you think as far back as you can, tell me one of your favorite memories.
Sue	When I was four or five, I had this imaginary place. It was a beautiful spot on the other side of a bridge. When my parents told me to do something that I didn't want to do, I just crossed over the bridge into that beautiful place.
Counselor	And what was the meaning of that place to you as a kid?
Sue	It was a place that I could go and be free and do anything I wanted to do in my imagination.
Counselor	And do you have a favorite TV show now?
Sue	I love all the reality shows . . . where they put people in exciting and challenging positions—way out of the ordinary.
Counselor	I'm beginning to get some pattern from the stories you are telling me. There's a strong theme of being free to do things that are out of the ordinary, allow a lot of freedom and variety, and may also present some risk. Are those characteristics that describe you?

Sue	Yes, quite well. If I could do some kind of work that would pick up on those themes, work would no longer be boring.
Counselor	Have you identified any such occupations?
Sue	No, because I've never thought about looking for occupations in that way. I am intrigued by the possibility of international business. I think that work in that field could offer the opportunity for a lot of travel, a lot of variety, and a chance to meet a lot of interesting people. And, it's not your common, everyday occupation.
Counselor	That's a good start. For our next session I want you to recall some other early memories so that you can tell me about them next week . . . and I want you to use this website (giving her a card with a web address on it) to find some other occupations that contain the kind of adventure, risk, and independence that you are looking for.

THEORY OF JOHN KRUMBOLTZ

Coming from the camp of learning theorists, John Krumboltz views a person's career choices and development through the perspective of the repertoire of behaviors he or she has been able to learn. Just as individuals have been able to learn the behaviors and skills they possess when they come to a counselor, they are capable of learning new ones if doing so would benefit their career development. Important roles for a counselor are to encourage exploratory behavior, teach new skills, and facilitate experiences that can result in new learning.

The foundational concepts of the theory are as follows:

- There are four primary determinants of career choice and development: genetic endowment, environmental conditions and events, instrumental and associative learning experiences, and knowledge of task approach skills (Krumboltz, 1996).
- It is not likely that counselors can have any impact on genetic endowment or environmental conditions; conversely, however, they can impact a client's future learning experiences and can teach what Krumboltz calls *task approach skills,* which are cognitive, decision-making skills.
- Holding irrational beliefs about career choices and development can serve as a significant barrier to setting goals and making satisfying choices. One significant role of a counselor is to assist the client to identify these irrational beliefs and combat them.
- Each individual filters events and information through his or her own self-observation and worldview generalizations. Thus, one's reality or view of the world is tempered by a personal belief system that has been learned in the environment.
- Learning and self-observation generalizations are powerfully impacted by positive reinforcement and/or positive role models. People learn as they are

positively reinforced for their attitudes or behaviors. They also learn as they model the behavior of role models. Counselors can use both positive reinforcement and positive role models to shape the behaviors of clients.

- Especially in the 21st century, uncertainty is an acceptable and positive condition. It can be used to catalyze exploration and to create opportunities for new learning. Counselors should focus on encouraging exploration and learning in clients rather than on helping them to reach the best solution or choose the "right" major or occupation.

COUNSELING GOALS AND STEPS

Within the Krumboltz framework, counseling goals include the following:

- identifying and removing irrational beliefs that affect career choice and development
- teaching decision-making and other task-approach skills, if these are lacking
- expanding the client's horizons of options by encouraging exploration and real-life experiences
- creating opportunities for the client to experience positive reinforcement for behaviors that are considered positive for the client
- creating opportunities for the client to adopt positive role models
- developing appropriate career planning skills (exploration, getting information, crystallizing choice, weighing options) that move the client toward self-selected goals
- assisting the client to accept uncertainty as a normal condition and to use it to plan new experiences and capitalize on what Krumboltz calls "happenstance."

Krumboltz and Baker (1973) identify the following eight steps in the career counseling relationship:

1. Define the problem and the client's goals.
2. Seek and get mutual agreement to achieve the goals.
3. Generate alternative problem solutions.
4. Collect information about these alternatives.
5. Examine the potential consequences of each alternative.
6. Reevaluate goals, alternatives, and consequences.
7. Make a decision or choice.
8. Generalize the decision-making process to new problems.

SAMPLE COUNSELOR–CLIENT INTERCHANGE

(The client has taken the Career Beliefs Inventory *prior to the first interview.)*

Counselor   Sue, please come on in. How are you today? And what would you like to discuss?

Sue	I'm in my sophomore year . . . I came to college to get enough education to get a better job. So far I've been taking the required courses, but I need to declare a major by the end of next semester.
Counselor	It's OK not to always have a specific plan, but it sounds as if you're bumping up against a deadline for making an important decision. What do you think you need to do or know to make this decision?
Sue	I need to have a lot of information about all the jobs I could enter and how the majors here at State relate to them.
Counselor	Yes, that would be a good start on solving this problem. Is there a reason why you haven't done that before?
Sue	I don't have a lot of confidence that I would know how to go about that. I thought you could help.
Counselor	I notice, from the results of the inventory you took, that you feel unsure about your ability to make decisions. Let's think about some important past decisions you have made, successful ones. Can you tell me about one?
Sue	I think I made a good decision about choosing this school.
Counselor	And why do you think so?
Sue	Well, being able to commute to a good school that doesn't cost too much and being able to keep my part-time job at the grocery store—all those things are meeting the needs that I have at this time in my life.
Counselor	So, the results of the decision you made are good for you—making it possible for you to reach your goal of getting a college degree. What kind of process did you use when you chose this school?
Sue	First, I got a list of all the schools within 50 miles of where I live. Then, I crossed off the private schools because they were too expensive. I also crossed off Central State University because I didn't have a high enough grade average in high school. That left me with just two schools. Finally, I visited both schools, talked to people in the admissions office, and talked to several people who had attended each school. Then, the choice became easy.
Counselor	It sounds as if you made a goal to go to college that was not too expensive and within easy driving distance so that you could get a college degree while keeping the part-time job you have. And then you did the right things after that. Sounds like good decision-making to me. Can we apply that same process to your next decision—choosing a major?
Sue	Yes, I guess so, but I just don't have any idea what occupations I should consider, except that I think that I'd like to work with people in some way.

Counselor	Have you had any experience in such jobs?
Sue	Yes, I have. In two of my jobs—receptionist and grocery store clerk—I dealt with people every day. I found that if I am pleasant with them, even if they are grumpy, and if I put myself out a little for them, they warm up to me and appreciate what I do. That gives me a good feeling. I'd like to work in a higher-paying job where I could work with people and get the satisfaction of knowing that I helped or served them in some way.
Counselor	Have you thought about what such jobs might be?
Sue	No, I haven't. I thought maybe you could help me.
Counselor	What other kinds of work or volunteer experience could you seek out so that you could explore other possibilities?
Sue	I just don't know.
Counselor	There is a website called *O*Net Online* that will allow you to choose groups of jobs such as human services, education, and health care services. You can use that site from here or from home. Once you choose a group, a list of occupations will be provided. When you ask for a description, you will get very detailed information about each occupation, including abilities and skills needed, typical activities, training needed, values the occupation may help you attain, and much more. This site could give you some ideas. This sheet gives you step-by-step instructions about what to select on each menu. When you come next week, please bring printouts of several jobs that interest you. Be sure to look at occupations you never heard of, as well as those whose names you recognize. Even though you think you would prefer jobs in which you work directly with people, explore some of the other groups, too.
Sue	What will I need to do after that?
Counselor	We'll look at the list together and decide whether there are other options that you might want to explore. After that, I'm going to suggest that you interview at least two people who work in the occupations you put in high priority. Because you don't have to declare a major for another semester, I'm also going to suggest that you take one or two sample courses in the major most closely related to the occupation you choose and that you seek out other experiences to work with people in ways that are different from the experience you've already had. Doing an internship related to your choices next semester would also be a good learning experience.
Sue	OK. I'll get busy learning about my options, and I'll make another appointment for next week. Thanks for bolstering my confidence that I can do this.

SUMMARY

In insufficient space, this chapter has reviewed three of the field's classic theories of career choice and development and has described a fourth approach that is more recent. Snippets of typical interviews with Sue, a fictitious case, have been presented in an effort to illustrate how each theory would be applied.

It is likely that most practicing career counselors would choose to be eclectic, that is, to select a theory and its accompanying techniques for a given client or situation. For example, Holland's theory might be selected for use with a client who has lost a job and needs help identifying other jobs that use a similar set of skills and interests. Super's theory might be selected if the need is to have a "skeleton" on which to design a career development program for students in grades 7–14. Savickas' approach might be selected for a client who talks freely and has good insight. Krumboltz' theory might be selected for work with a client who needs to learn decision-making skills and would profit from experiential learning.

Further, multiple theories may be applied to one case. For example, a counselor dealing with Sue from multiple theoretical perspectives might use Holland's theory and assessment to assist her to identify occupations and majors; Krumboltz's theory to engineer learning experiences to enhance her self-concept and aid in reality testing; Super's Career Rainbow and related assessments to plan for future life roles; and a constructivist, narrative approach to shortening a list of occupational options and making an action plan. In short, each theoretical perspective examines the phenomenon of career choice and development through a different lens and forms a different kaleidoscopic pattern. In actuality, all of these theories (and others) can be integrated into one that provides a broader perspective than any single theory can.

Context and Career Planning

- **Internal Variables**
- **External Variables**

Izuma is a 30-year-old Japanese woman who became an American citizen through marriage. When she came to the United States to live with her husband, she expressed her long-term desire to enter graduate school. Because, however, she was uncertain about her career goals, and therefore her area of specialty in graduate school, she sought the help of a counselor at the university counseling center.

The counselor, after hearing Izuma's statement of the reason for counseling, spent the remainder of the first interview gathering data to help him understand the external variables that could be influential in Izuma's decision making. He learned that Izuma was the only child of a father who is an engineer and a mother who, following the Japanese tradition, had never worked outside the home. Izuma had lived in the United States during two four-year intervals in her life when her father was assigned to Honda plants in the United States. She, therefore, had a good command of English and knowledge of the American culture. Izuma felt a lot of pressure from her parents and Japanese society to get married rather than to continue in the administrative assistant position she had with a large company in Tokyo. Her American husband is supportive of her desire to go to graduate school and to pursue a career.

After this initial interview, the counselor asked Izuma to take two inventories on the Internet: the Kuder Career Search with Person Match and the Super Work Values Inventory. Results of the interest inventory showed high interest in two clusters: the Personal/Social cluster (95th percentile) and the Sales/Management cluster (92nd percentile), that is, a very high interest in working with people either to help them in some way or to lead and manage them. On Super's Work Values Inventory, the highest three values were achievement, prestige, and independence. In discussion about the differences between the work tasks and the characteristics of these two clusters, it became obvious that, despite the high measured interest in the Sales and Management cluster and potential to attain the most important work values in it, occupations of this kind could not be seriously considered by Izuma. The expectations for women in their culture were that they would be passive, supportive, and serving the needs of others.

The counselor then assisted Izuma to learn about the occupations in the Personal/Social cluster that require a graduate degree. Izuma decided to enter a master's degree program in counseling and to attempt to attain her values of prestige, achievement, and independence through a career plan that would lead to a management position in the counseling field.

As with Izuma, career development, choice, and change always take place within the context of the person and the environment. In career choices, that context always involves the internal reality of the decider and the external reality of the world of work. Parsons (1909), father of career counseling, laid groundwork for our consideration of these two contextual entities in his statement of a three-step process, as follows:

1. Develop a clear understanding of yourself, your attitudes, abilities, interests, ambitions, resource limitations, and other qualities;
2. Develop a knowledge of the requirements and conditions of success, advantages and disadvantages, compensation, opportunities, and prospects in different lines of work;
3. Use "true reasoning" on the relations of these two groups of facts (p. 5).

FIGURE 3.1 The archway of career determinants

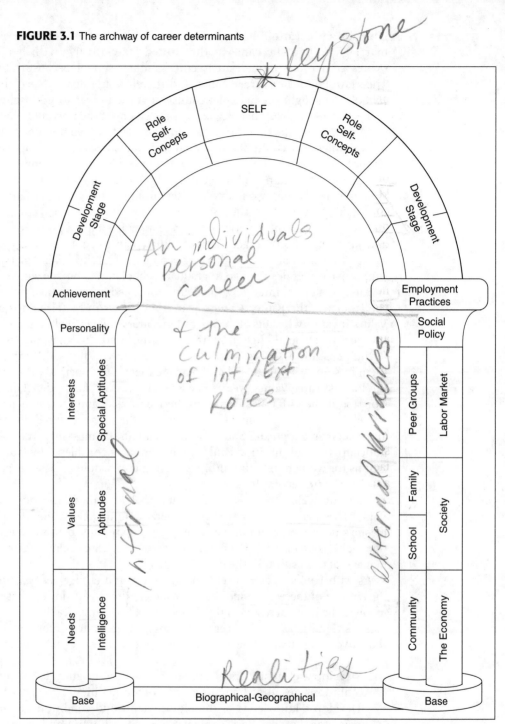

Source: From Career Choice and Development: Applying Contemporary Theories to Practice (2nd ed.).
Duane Brown, Linda Brooks, and Assoc. (Eds.), Copyright © 1990, Jossey-Bass Inc. This material is used by
permission of Jossey-Bass Inc., a subsidiary of John Wiley & Sons, Inc.

Super (1990), at the other end of the 20th century, summed up this concept in his Archway of Determinants, as shown in Figure 3.1. This graphic, provided as a visual image of the career development process, was Super's last contribution to the field before his death. In this image he attempted to weave together his earlier work on developmental life stages and tasks, self-concept, and the Life Career Rainbow.

Let's begin by looking at the top of the graphic. The archway at the top represents an individual's personal career and is the culmination of the interaction of internal and external variables depicted by its two pillars. Notice that the archway is in the shape of the Life-Career Rainbow (see Chapter 2, page 21). Its building blocks are developmental stages and life roles across the life span. Notice that the keystone of that personal career is the self, as expressed through a vocational self-concept, perhaps a visual expression of Super's statement that the choice of an occupation is the implementation of a self-concept.

The base of the graphic represents biographical and geographical realities. In Super's model, the biographical aspects probably equate to one's personal life story—the sequence of life events and influences that have molded an individual's needs, values, interests, and aptitudes. These biographical realities include gender, race, socioeconomic class, family values, and the like.

The geographic reality includes ethnic and cultural influences on an individual and the availability of and access to options in a given place. Different cultures have different expectations about the roles of men and women. Some cultures expect their youth to pursue the same occupational choices as their parents. Some allow free choice to their citizens while others expect their citizens to enter those occupations dictated by labor market need or test scores. Some cultures expect a long extended career in the same occupation with the same company, while others offer freedom of career movement and the opportunity to gain additional education or skill at any time in life. There is evidence of the influence of both of these kinds of factors on Izuma's career perspectives and choices. The influence of culture is truly a major one related to an individual's career choice and development.

These two foundational concepts give rise to two equal columns that support and feed into an individual's personal career choice: *internal variables* in the left column and *external variables* in the right column. These two columns include the primary factors that blend to form the context in which clients make their career choices.

INTERNAL VARIABLES

When providing counseling assistance, career counselors tend to focus more on the internal variables of a person than on the external variables. The first of these internal variables included on the Arch of Determinants is *needs*. Roe (1956), basing her work largely on Maslow's (1954) hierarchy of needs, proposed that psychological needs are developed through parent–child interactions in early childhood. These may result in the need to work with people rather than with things or technology, for example. Roe classified occupations by eight areas of interest that relate to needs formed by parent–child interactions and by six levels of educational entry, which have a correlation with Maslow's hierarchy of needs. Roe hypothesized that Maslow's lower-order needs (for food, shelter, clothing, and safety, for example) could be met by occupations that can be entered at the lowest levels of education (high school or less), but that higher-order needs (belonging, esteem, information, understanding, beauty, and self-actualization) would be met by occupations requiring varying levels of postsecondary education.

In spite of the lack of research support for Roe's theory of psychological needs and the effect of parent–child interactions in early childhood, it is commonly accepted in career development theory and practice that individuals do have varying needs and that some of those needs can be entirely or partially filled through work.

The second internal variable on the Archway is *intelligence*. Heredity bestows on each individual a level of intelligence. In general, these levels have determining power over the amount and kind of education one can complete and, therefore, on the level of occupation one can pursue. Roe's classification system, well supported by research, is helpful here. That system proposed six levels: professional and managerial 1, professional and managerial 2, semiprofessional, skilled, semiskilled, and unskilled. All occupations can be organized into these six levels. More recently, occupations in the O*Net (US Department of Labor, 2007) database have been classified into five job zones, levels of education ranging from completion of high school or less to completion of a graduate degree. Thus, the intelligence and the motivation to achieve a specific level of education serve as one determinant of career choice. Besides the genetic endowment that parents provide, they also have a very significant influence on goals and motivation for educational attainment.

A third internal variable on the Archway is *values*. Holland (1997) proposes that individuals can be categorized by personality types, that those of a given type pursue skills to support their type and, at a later age, take on a set of values consistent with that personality type. Brown (1996) proposes that values are the driving force behind career choices, as individuals seek to attain their values through work. Super (1980) also proposed that values are strong determinants of career choices and that values may be allocated across life roles for their attainment. Through his international Work Importance Study, Super identified 12 values that are common across cultures—such as variety, achievement, high income, security, and prestige. Being able to attain one's most important values is critical to life satisfaction. The importance of these values can be measured by taking the Super Work Values Inventory (Kuder & Zytowski, 2007). A fourth category of internal variables is *interests*. Holland (1997) posits that interests are formed because parents and other influential adults offer activities to children and that those activities that are positively reinforced become interests. Further, he proposes that people seek occupations or jobs that utilize their interests and that individuals will be most satisfied in work that is attuned to those interests. The formation of interests begins in the middle school years, and interests become more and more stable across the life span. There are many reliable and valid inventories that measure the interests of individuals and provide a list of occupations related to the client's interests. Interests can also be identified through a structured interview. A fifth category of internal variables is *aptitudes*, a predisposition to be able to learn skills and be proficient in specific areas, such as language, mathematics, spatial relations, and mechanical reasoning. Groups of occupations, arranged by the Roe eight clusters or the Holland six clusters, clearly require different sets of skills, which result from the application of aptitudes. Aptitudes can be measured by timed, standardized instruments such as the Differential Aptitude Tests (Harcourt Assessment, 1990) or the O*Net Abilities Profiler (US Department of Labor, 1999). Skills—a finer breakdown of aptitudes—can be measured through instruments in which the client rates himself or herself on multiple skills, as in the Kuder Skills Assessment (Kuder Inc., 2006), or by more formal instruments, such as ACT's WorkKeys (ACT Inc., 2007).

The combination and interaction of these variables—needs, intelligence, values, interests, and aptitudes—result in a unique personality for each individual, and each person makes career choices within the context of his or her unique personality. That unique personality is expressed as the *self-concept*. According to Super, people seek to implement their unique self-concepts through work and other life roles. As noted at the top of the Archway of Determinants, it is the self-concept that serves as the keystone of one's personal career development.

ASSESSING SELF-VARIABLES

Career counselors may use a variety of techniques to identify self-variables for a given client. Those techniques include the use of formal assessment tools—such as inventories of interests, needs, values, and personality types—and tests of aptitude or achievement. They also include informal assessment techniques such as interviewing, checklists, career fantasy, and analysis of life stories.

From some combination of these techniques and tools, counselors help themselves and their clients to put together a picture of self (which Super called *psychtalk*) which can be translated into occupational options (which Super called *occtalk*). Companion to this process is the development of a desired personal career rainbow (combination of life roles) and the allocation of interests, values, and skills to various life roles.

EXTERNAL VARIABLES

The right-hand column of the Arch of Determinants addresses the variables that, according to this graphic, are of equal importance when molding career development and choice for individuals. These variables have their roots in geography, that is, they relate to race, ethnicity, and physical location.

The first of these is the *economy*. When the economy is booming, there are many more job openings than when the economy is lagging. This fact has the effect of making it easier for individuals to find and keep jobs. Employers, including the military and government, may need to lower the bar of usual admission requirements or selectivity in order to get enough people into the workforce. The U.S. Immigration and Naturalization Services (INS) may increase the number of foreigners who are allowed to enter the United States on work visas. Ex-offenders and other hard-to-place categories of workers may be able to find jobs. Some sectors of the economy may be growing so rapidly that there is an unusually high job demand in specific occupations, making it possible to enter these with less training than typical and/or at higher salaries.

The second of these is the *community,* including the *family.* Community can be defined as all those who directly surround an individual. Under this definition, the community for a given person is comprised of family members, neighbors, coworkers, friends, and acquaintances. It is a well-known fact that parents and other family members are the greatest influencers of vocational choice. Thus, when dealing with a client it is important to learn what these influences are and to understand the educational and vocational pressures and expectations that may come from family and friends. For example, most parents transmit the notion that going to a four-year college and entering occupations that require that kind of education is somehow better than going to vocational-technical training and entering its associated occupations. In some racial or ethnic groups, men and women are expected to play certain roles and to enter certain kinds of occupations. Similarly, membership in a specific racial or ethnic group may mean that the client holds values that are different from those of the dominant culture. For example, African-American, Asian, or Hispanic persons may value career choices that contribute to the family welfare more than those that contribute only to personal well-being. Members of some racial and ethnic groups value time with family over time for work. Membership in a racial or ethnic group alone is not a determiner that an individual will subscribe to the values of the group. Thus, career counselors must understand how the values of different racial-ethnic groups vary from the norms of the dominant culture, and must determine what the client's level of acculturation to the dominant culture is. Role models are important influencers on career choice and should also be considered in the mix of community influences.

A third external influence is *society in general.* This is the remainder of humankind beyond the community. Society imposes stereotypes, for example, about appropriate occupations for men and women, for gay people and straight people, for young and old, for obese and slim, and for those of racial-ethnic diversity. Society also gives messages about which jobs have higher prestige than others, which deserve higher salaries than others, and which levels of education or specific colleges are better than others. Society also dictates how its disenfranchised—the disabled, mentally challenged, ex-offenders, and the poor—will be accepted into the workplace, in what kinds of jobs, and what levels of benefits. That same society decides whether to equally accept members of all religious faiths or to discriminate against some.

Especially for adolescents and young adults, the fourth influence, *peer group,* is powerful. The peer group has a strong influence on the occupations and schools that young people consider as options. The values of that peer group, which often favors high income and all that it can buy, may become those of an individual facing career choices, especially before the onset of adulthood. Similarly, the influence of the parents' peer group is reflected through the influences of parents on their children.

The fifth influence, *the labor market,* is also a powerful influence on career choices. In the 21st century, there are many rapid changes in the labor market.

Occupations are being added and deleted at a fast pace, as technology does more and more of the tasks once done by humans. This, in turn, creates new jobs to support the technology. As a result of this trend, manufacturing assembly-line jobs continue to be on the decline (as are jobs in retail sales). Manufacturing has been severely impacted because jobs previously done by people are now more efficiently done by computers and robots. The number of workers needed in retail sales has declined because of the combination of TV and Internet sales and the advent of the huge, low staff warehouse chains. Current projections of the U.S. Department of Labor indicate that approximately 65% of the jobs in the early 21st century will require up to two years of education or training beyond high school, while only 20% will require a bachelor's degree or higher—a changed picture from that of the 20th century.

The same technologies that have made some occupations obsolete have created others, though in much smaller numbers. The rise of the World Wide Web has created jobs for webmasters, website developers, and programmers while it has reduced jobs for letter carriers (and other types of postal workers), retail sales workers, and clerical workers. The rapid rise in the use of cellular phones has increased the demand for telemarketers and cellular tower builders, but it has eliminated jobs for switchboard operators and line installers and repair people.

Similarly, the same technologies have vastly modified the work tasks of a myriad of occupations. Consider the difference in the way that bank tellers, secretaries, teachers, accountants, and auto mechanics do their work today as compared to ten years ago. Because of rapid changes in the work tasks of occupations and the potential short life of an occupation, workers of the 21st century will need to continually update their skills. Further, more emphasis will be given to considering one's combination of skills than to selecting an occupation. Skills will be transferable from one occupation to another, as is already illustrated by the fact that the Department of Labor's *O*Net* (the replacement for the former *Dictionary of Occupational Titles*) describes occupations by the skill set required as well as by the job duties.

The place in which people work may also be vastly different as the labor market changes. In the 21st century, significant numbers of people will work from home, linking themselves to coworkers and managers through the Internet with its capability of email and videoconferencing. The trend of entrepreneurship will continue with more and more people making their living through private businesses that may be either geographically or virtually based.

The impact of the labor market includes new and changing occupations, shifting amounts of need for people in different occupations, and changing *employment practices,* a sixth variable. In the 20th century, an employee expected to work for the same employer for a long period of time and to have a good package of fringe benefits. In the 21st century, employees will change jobs many more times than in the 20th century, because employers have a changed mentality. That mentality is to keep an employee so long as the organization needs his or her skills, but no longer, due to the constant scrutiny of the bottom line. The organization will be kept as trim as possible, with few middle managers. Rifkin (1995) talks about the existence of two groups in the information age: (1) a small, elite knowledge group that possesses management and technical skills and (2) disposable line workers. Another part of the new mentality is to hire "just-in-time workers" or contract workers rather than full-time employees who receive a good wage and a complete fringe benefits package. Employers may send routine work tasks to less-developed countries, where they can be done at a much lower per-hour cost. The combination of these labor market conditions makes it increasingly difficult for underskilled, poorly educated, or disabled workers to find jobs.

SUMMARY

The career development and choice process is a very complex one that emerges from the interaction of multiple variables: both internal and external. Internal variables that counselors must assist clients to assess are intelligence, needs, values, abilities, interests, ethnic-cultural background, religious commitment, and physical condition. Ideally and theoretically, identifying occupations and a specific working environment whose characteristics match the characteristics of the person would lead to job satisfaction and a positive contribution. Yet, applying such a systematic, trait-and-factor approach fails to consider the power of external variables. The rapidly changing economy, social policies, structure of the world of work, and employment practices will have an effect on every individual career choice; as will the influence of family, community, and society in general.

C H A P T E R

Negotiating the Career Counseling Relationship

- **Creating a Mattering Climate**
- **Building Bridges**
- **Negotiating the Working Alliance**
- **Coping with Client Reluctance**

The importance of the relationship is something that is recognized in most career counseling theories. There are differences with respect to how much emphasis is placed on the relationship, but there is general agreement that the formation of a healthy relationship is an integral part of the career counseling process (Tursi & Cochran, 2006). Through the relationship, clients rebuild their self-confidence and find within themselves the strength to trust and use their personal abilities (Bohart & Tallman, 1999).

Despite the agreement on the importance of the relationship, there is considerable variation with respect to what it actually means to build a good relationship with a client. In some situations, people assume that a sentence or two is all that is needed. While this certainly is a beginning, the building of the relationship is far more involved. In many respects, the relationship acts as a foundation for everything else that follows. Without a solid foundation there is very little that can be accomplished. Kelly (1997) uses the relationship as an integrating concept that combines and unifies many of the humanistic and technical components of counseling.

When discussing the various facets of the relationship, there are many different images that can be used to discuss how the relationship fits with other helping processes. In some respects, the idea of a "stage" of development is helpful because it communicates the necessity of building something before going on to problem solving. While this image is helpful it also is more static than what we would like to communicate. The relationship certainly provides a foundation, but it does not have a definite ending point. The relationship continues to develop throughout all aspects of career counseling. In many ways it is like a spiral, there is a certain level of relationship established at the beginning, but with the passage of time this relationship deepens and moves to another level. It is not something that you establish and then move on, it is always a part of the career counseling process.

Carl Rogers (1951, 1961, 1989), probably more than any other theorist, has laid a solid foundation for the formation of the counseling relationship. He suggested that the key counseling conditions should be genuineness, unconditional positive regard, and empathic understanding. Within this client-centered framework the counselor is a facilitator rather than an "expert." There is also an emphasis on tolerance and making an effort to understand the experiential world of the other person.

We want to assert the importance of the relationship, but also must examine what this actually means when put into practice. Relationship building requires certain actions and attitudes. It is our intention to outline some ways of facilitating this process.

CREATING A MATTERING CLIMATE

Another way to approach the counseling relationship is by examining "mattering," the degree to which people feel that they are important (they matter). Schlossberg, Lynch, and Chickering (1989) define mattering as the "beliefs people have, whether right or wrong, that they matter to someone else, that they are the object of someone else's attention, and that others care about them and appreciate them." A sense of mattering is a key ingredient in the helping relationship.

Schlossberg, Lynch, and Chickering (1989) suggest that there are several different levels of mattering. The first level focuses on basic *visibility,* just being noticed by another person. The power of visibility can be appreciated if you consider what it feels like to be ignored (to be invisible). Some people express their anger by ignoring or looking past the other person. At a very basic level, we all have the desire to be noticed. One of the experiences associated with unemployment and the job search is that of invisibility. People looking for work enter offices and often find themselves being actively ignored, particularly when their intentions become known. People busy themselves with work while the job seeker stands at the counter.

In the counseling office, clients must be noticed as soon as they enter the premises. The expression of acknowledgment is not something that rests solely on the shoulders of the counselor. All staff have a role to play in establishing a mattering climate within the office. Mattering is something that starts with the first contact between the client and the office staff and it carries forward as an important ingredient in the counseling relationship.

An interesting exercise is to just sit in a counseling office and watch people as they enter and receive service. How are they treated by staff? What is the process for receiving service? As you cast your eyes about the office, pay attention to the way in which the physical space is organized. How is the waiting area and the offices constructed? What information is on the walls? As you make these observations, think critically about the messages that are being communicated by the physical and the organizational structures.

A second level of mattering occurs when you not only notice the person but also extend to them a sense of real *importance.* To appreciate what is involved at this level, think about what happens when a person you consider to be important pays a visit. The important person is usually greeted at the door, they are escorted to a comfortable chair, a drink is offered, and people listen carefully to them when they speak. How does this compare to how counseling clients are typically handled? Are counselors extending social graces, or are they following a medical model of relationship building? The medical model is often organized in such a way to reduce mattering and to establish a clear hierarchy of importance. We believe that much could be gained by returning to more of a social model of interpersonal communication.

Another important aspect of communicating importance is to take the time to listen carefully to the person's story. Listening is an essential part of career counseling, and it is important to allow sufficient time to hear the whole story. Sometimes counselors get ahead of themselves and try to move ahead to problem solving before they have heard the full story. Listening to the story is important for information, but it is also a significant way of communicating to another person that they are important—they matter.

Moving to the third level of mattering, there is the opportunity for people to *offer help* as well as to receive it. People feel they matter when they feel that what they have to contribute is really valued and needed. Think about a situation in which you felt that others really needed your help. The feeling of being needed serves as a strong motivator. In the counseling relationship, however, there is a tendency to concentrate the help in only one direction. While it is true that clients need help, they also benefit from opportunities to help others. One of the advantages of group counseling is that clients can help one another. As career counselors, we need to challenge ourselves to find ways that clients can give as well as receive help.

The highest level of mattering occurs when clients truly believe that they have a *personal* and *professional* relationship with the counselor. At this level, clients believe that the counselor genuinely cares about their well-being and that this care is more than just a professional role that they are assuming. They believe, for example, that the counselor will continue to be interested in them even after they have stopped being a client. Care at this level is something that is greater than just what is happening within career counseling sessions. In extending this form of mattering the counselor has to go the "extra mile." In one challenging situation, the client had to go to the hospital for a minor operation. The counselor phoned afterwards to check on the health and well-being of the client. This one phone call had a major impact on the creation of a strong mattering relationship.

A full expression of mattering requires actions as well as intentions. The acronym PLEASE can be used to illustrate some of the many ways of expressing mattering.

P—**protecting.** Providing a secure and safe haven for exploratory efforts. Ensuring that clients receive all of the benefits to which they are entitled.

L—**listening.** Taking the time to hear all aspects of a person's story. Paying attention to underlying feelings while they tell the story.

E—**enquiring.** Expressing interest in the story through questions and requests for clarification. Being naturally curious and asking about events in the person's life.

A—**acknowledging.** Noticing the other person and expressing greetings both verbally and nonverbally.

S—**supporting.** Expressing encouragement and praise. Identifying positive attitudes and behaviors and providing specific feedback.

E—**exchanging.** Sharing information about oneself. This self-disclosure should be genuine and appropriate to the situation.

Mattering is something that not only exists between client and counselor, it is also a feeling that occurs between career counseling staff and management. It is often easier for career counselors to express mattering to clients when they feel a sense of mattering within the organization. One of the ways of increasing mattering for clients is to improve the working climate of the counselors. There seems to be a parallel process: when counselors feel good about themselves and their workplace, they are better able to extend mattering to others (Amundson, 1993).

The concept of mattering is receiving increasing amounts of attention in the counseling literature (Corbierre & Amundson, 2007; Dixon Rayle, 2006; Elliott, Kao, & Grant, 2004). Given the importance of the relationship in determining a positive counseling outcome, it is important that counselors focus more energy on ways of strengthening the counseling relationship.

BUILDING BRIDGES

Another important aspect of relationship building is the establishment of connections, or bridges, between the clients and the counselors. Clients are interested in telling their stories, but also want to be assured that the counselors can understand and appreciate their life circumstances (Amundson, Westwood, & Prefontaine, 1995). While counselors may have some technical expertise, can they really appreciate what is happening in the lives of their clients. One of the ways that counselors can express their understanding is through drawing parallels and connections between themselves and their clients. These linkages reinforce client-counselor bonds if they are handled in an appropriate manner.

This sharing of personal experiences is something that can be contained within certain limits. Counselors often joke about a counselor who responds to the client's problems by saying, "You think you have problems, just listen to mine." What is required is a balanced approach to listening to client problems and forming linkages through appropriate counselor self-disclosure.

Discovering areas of linkage and common ground requires a broad understanding of the client's life circumstances. This means taking the time to enquire about more than the client's presenting problem (a good mattering strategy). Clients often come to career counseling prepared to launch into a lengthy description of the problem. It can be helpful to stop this process and suggest that, before getting into the problem, it might be helpful to just get to know one another.

One way of facilitating this initial interaction is to use a structured activity for which the client is encouraged to take a blank piece of paper and write down up to 20 things that they enjoy doing (Amundson, 2003a, 2003b). After she has compiled her list, she is asked to think about each activity with respect to some of the following dimensions: (1) When did she last engage in the activity? (2) What are the costs associated with the activity? (3) Is the activity something she does alone or with others? (4) Is the activity something that is spontaneous or is planning involved? and (5) How does the activity meet her physical, mental, emotional, or spiritual needs? By having clients develop this overview of activities, the career counselor generates a broad range of topics for further exploration and discussion. The breadth of these activities is such that it allows for a more holistic exploration. Rather than just focusing on the problem, the counselor can extend the exploration to other areas. This broader consideration is helpful when counselors are trying to identify other interests or other areas of strength.

In order to use the above activity effectively it is important that counselors start by creating their own list (it's always a good idea to try out the activity yourself before using it with clients). Counselors can then make links by referring to their own list of activities. For example, a career counselor might say something like the following to build a connection:

Counselor	When I did my list I also put down riding a bike as a key interest area. Where do you ride your bike?
Client	I like riding through the mountain trails.

Counselor	I usually ride on the flatlands. Tell me more about some of your adventures on the mountain trails.

These small connections can help to strengthen the bond between counselor and clients.

Building common ground is particularly important in situations where there are significant differences in culture, age, gender, disability, education level, religion, economic status, sexual orientation, and so on (Weinrach & Thomas, 1996). While there are differences, there also are many similarities that need to be acknowledged. It is important to focus on both similarities and differences, and through this process ensure that counseling becomes a more humane endeavor.

When building bridges with clients, there is usually a need to ask personal questions, as well as a more traditional set of career questions. The question often becomes where to set the boundaries. Career counselors often are much more conservative in the questions they ask than the clients they serve. This conservatism is more a reflection of counselor anxieties than client needs. Areas of discussion should be wide-ranging and thus make reference to ideas, to feelings, to actions or behaviors, and to spiritual perspectives. As might be expected, the area where there is often the greatest reluctance for discussion is the spiritual domain. For many clients, spiritual matters might be at the heart of their career concerns. Counselors need to be willing to ask about spiritual perspectives in an appropriate and respectful manner. Within each of these areas there may be opportunities to build bridges.

NEGOTIATING THE WORKING ALLIANCE

When clients and career counselors come together, there is usually a need to negotiate and establish the roles that each will assume within the relationship. There can be issues of confidentiality and there also might be some suspicions because of past experiences and sanctions that might be applied. Whatever the starting point, it is important to have a clear and frank discussion at the beginning about expectations and roles. Once this basic process has been clarified, there is room to explore and develop other aspects of the relationship. Through this negotiated engagement the relationship is built and the working relationship is created.

An important aspect of the working alliance is the alignment of client and career counselor goals. Both the client and the career counselor enter the counseling relationship with certain expectations about what is going to happen. Many clients assume that the counselor has some "magical tricks" that will solve all their problems. Perhaps there is a special test, or some hidden knowledge, that will reveal the answers to their questions. Career counselors, on the other hand, also have their expectations about the process and the activities that will be used. Clients may assume that career counselors will do all the work and will solve their problems for them, but counselors usually have much different ideas.

As a guide to help you look at roles and different expectations, consider the following metaphoric possibilities:

1. coach (direct, support, teach)
2. gardener (nurture, support, prune, pull weeds)
3. lifeguard (observe, react, save)
4. reframing agent (creative, influence, act)
5. Santa Claus (positive, giving bountiful gifts)
6. parent (nurture, guide, support)
7. doctor (listen, analyze, prescribe)
8. craftsperson (creative, practical, skillful)
9. manager (organize, implement policies, support)
10. team player (practice, collaborate, play the game)
11. salesperson (influence, market)
12. programmer (understand the rules, designer)
13. lobbyist (advocate, influential, behind the scenes)
14. analyst (assess, solve puzzles)
15. security guard (check, enforce rules)
16. travel agent (listen, sales, match people with destinations)
17. spokesperson (advocate, visible, representative)

You can use this list of roles, and others if you wish, to think about your own views of career counseling. Which roles do you see yourself playing in the career counseling situation (you can play multiple roles)? How do the roles you are choosing fit with the role expectations of your clients? You might want to use this list of roles with your clients, as a way of discussing different expectations about career counseling roles.

One of the common misconceptions about the career counseling process is the amount of time needed to do effective career planning. Clients often underestimate the time needed, and it can be helpful to use the image of a career wheel as a framework for discussion.

The career wheel is outlined in Figure 4.1 (Amundson & Poehnell, 1996). The development of career goals (the center of wheel) depends on input from each of the components of the wheel. Career choice is a complex process and depends upon a broad array of information. (Note: Chapters 6 and 7 provide illustrations of how to acquire information about the various components in the wheel.) By using the wheel for discussion and exploration purposes, the client is better prepared to collaboratively contribute to the counseling process.

As one illustration of how to use the wheel, consider situations where clients are looking to you, their career counselor, as someone can provide quick answers about which career direction they should be pursuing. By showing the career wheel, you have the opportunity to explain more about the process. You can also suggest that you would be happy to provide an opinion, once all the various segments of the wheel have been completed. From our experience, once the wheel has been completed there is usually a much better basis for having the discussion about career direction.

FIGURE 4.1 Career wheel

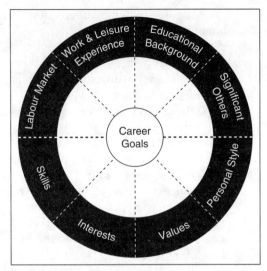

Source: From Career Pathways, *by Norman Amundson and Gray Poehnell, Copyright © 1996, Ergon Communications. This material is used by permission of Ergon Communications.*

COPING WITH CLIENT RELUCTANCE

Some clients come to career counseling with a certain degree of reluctance. Under these conditions, building a positive client–counselor relationship can be a challenge. The first step in approaching this challenge is to try to understand some of the underlying reasons behind the reluctant behavior. Descriptions of some common sources of reluctance are given in the following discussion.

FEAR OF THE UNFAMILIAR

For many clients, reluctance can simply be an expression of their unfamiliarity with the career counseling process. There are many myths about what happens in counseling. As such, it is only natural that some people are cautious about entering into the counseling relationship. Some people have the impression that career counselors are like magicians who analyze and form judgments about every statement that is made. Others worry about confidentiality and how information will be shared with others.

Whatever the source of concern, it can be helpful to ask at the start about what prior knowledge and expectations they have about career counseling. This is when to introduce some information and discussion about roles and responsibilities during the career counseling process.

REFUSAL TO ACKNOWLEDGE OR TAKE RESPONSIBILITY FOR THE PROBLEM

There are many social taboos about "having personal problems." Going to see a career counselor can be viewed as a sign of weakness. With this perspective, problems can be hidden or misrepresented. There can be an initial show of bravado and an unwillingness to openly discuss real issues.

It is impossible to help someone who won't acknowledge the need for help. At the same time, a breakthrough often comes after the person has had an opportunity to build a relationship. Sometimes it just takes time! One of the advantages of career counseling is that often it is easier to frame problems as career issues rather than as personal problems.

JOB LOSS AND JOB SEARCH BURNOUT

Studies of the dynamics of unemployment point to the existence of an emotional roller coaster (Borgen & Amundson, 1987). This time of emotional turmoil brings forth many different reactions. There are times at the beginning when people feel strong and don't feel that they need any help. At other times, there are feelings of loss (shock, anger, worry, or anxiety) or burnout (discouragement, stagnation, anger, desperation, or fear). Under these changing emotional conditions, there can be expressions of reluctance associated with the counseling process.

Being on an emotional roller coaster can be a frightening experience for clients. It can be helpful for counselors to acknowledge these feelings and to normalize some of the reactions associated with the experience. There is considerable variation in how people go through the unemployment experience, and it can be helpful for clients to realize that what they are experiencing is normal.

FIGHTING THE SYSTEM

Some clients have had previous negative experiences with counselors in other agencies. Coming for career counseling can be a reminder of problems they faced in the past. Based on these prior experiences, there can be some wariness about counselors and the counseling process.

It can be helpful to openly discuss some of the prior experiences with other counselors and with other agencies. It is usually better to have this information out in the open for dialogue purposes. There may be some similarities, but there also might be some important differences that need to be discussed.

SECONDARY GAINS

Depending on the situation, there may be some perceived threat to financial benefits (unemployment benefits, social assistance, support payments) from being too forthcoming in the counseling process. There also may be some advantage to presenting information in a manner that will justify extra support for educational or living expenses. It is not surprising that a certain amount of reluctance might be associated with these realities.

This is another situation where openness and dialogue are essential starting points. It is not always possible to set this aside, but at least there is an open recognition and discussion of rights and obligations.

MANDATED PARTICIPATION

There are many situations where the entry into career counseling is a mandated experience. For some young people, there is the situation where parents decide that "enough is enough" and some type of career counseling is needed. At a more formal level, there are situations in which clients have to receive career counseling in order to qualify for benefits. Under these circumstances it is not surprising to see the development of some reluctance. What is surprising is that this reluctance is often not as widespread as one might think. Based on our experience, it is possible to work with many of these clients as long as there is open communication and the demonstration of mattering in the career counseling situation. With the mandated client, it is important to turn the situation from one of power and control to one of mutual readiness and respect (Amundson & Borgen, 2000; Muscat, 2005). Sometimes a comment such as the following helps set the stage for this type of relationship:

> We are scheduled to spend three sessions together and I think we can accomplish some important tasks during this time. How we spend the time, however, is completely up to you. Let me know what would be most helpful.

There are certain guiding principles for working with reluctant clients. These principles can be applied to all the situations that have been described (Amundson & Borgen, 2000). These principles are as follows:

Principle One—Nondefensive Open Discussion

It is important to allow a period of venting and to encourage an open and frank discussion. When framing this discussion, it is important to treat clients with respect, to offer support, to make a clear offer of service, and to allow clients choice over issues where there is some flexibility. There are certain boundaries that must be respected. These boundaries focus on issues of confidentiality and respect for one another (Carroll, 1997).

Principle Two—Empathy

Many people who are expressing reluctance find themselves dealing with many strong emotions. These emotions need to be actively acknowledged and validated through the use of empathy (Miller & Rollnick, 2002). When the counselor uses empathy skills, clients feel more understood and appreciated (Abu Baker, 1999; Tretheway, 1997). When using these skills, it is important to be respectful (not patronizing) and to normalize the emotions that are being expressed.

Principle Three—Roles and Responsibilities

Most clients do not fully understand the roles and responsibilities associated with various helping professionals. Given this situation, it can be helpful to clarify counseling roles as well as to explain what is expected from clients (Newman, 1994; Maher et al., 1994). There are certain rights and obligations associated with the counseling process. Giving information and addressing misconceptions can play an important part in building a good relationship.

Principle Four—Walking Alongside

As much as possible, counselors need to communicate their interest in playing a supportive role in the helping process (Bischoff & Tracey, 1995). While there certainly can be some "control" functions associated with the counseling process, for the most part, career counseling should be a source of encouragement and support. Career counselors need to openly communicate their intention to try to understand each situation from the client's perspective (nonjudgmental).

In working with mandated clients the issue of being mandated needs to be addressed and resolved before it is possible to move forward. Very little can be accomplished if clients are unwilling to engage in the career counseling process. This often means spending more time at the beginning processing relationship issues.

SUMMARY

In this chapter we stress the importance of the counseling relationship. In the beginning, there is a need to focus on the relationship and to work toward the establishment of a positive working alliance. The relationship is something that needs to be negotiated and supported throughout the career counseling process.

Building the counseling relationship requires actions and attitudes that contribute to a mattering climate. Clients need to feel that they are important, valued, and integral to the success of career counseling. The relationship must be based on genuine caring and a willingness to share personal stories and to seek areas of common ground.

The establishment of the counseling relationship can be challenging. Career counselors need to understand some of the underlying dynamics of client reluctance and must work toward building more positive relationships. This can be achieved by engaging clients in nondefensive open discussions, where there is an expression of empathy and the sharing of information about roles and responsibilities. The basic motivation is always to walk alongside clients in an atmosphere of encouragement and support.

CHAPTER 5

Defining the Client's Career Concerns

- **Elaborating the Problem**
- **Viewing the Problem Through a Metaphoric Lens**
- **Changing Direction**

After establishing the initial working relationship, the focus shifts to the problem that needs to be addressed. Most clients are more than willing to begin telling their story. In instances where some encouragement is needed, a statement such as the following is helpful: "So what would you like to focus on today?" This question is designed to move the discussion from relationship building to a more direct focus on the problem.

When addressing the problem, people will often use stories to describe their situation. Imbedded within the story is the problem or problems that they would like to address. The challenge for the career counselor is to clearly identify the issues that need to be considered. Patsula (1992) suggests that one way to clarify the problems that have been described is to use constraint statements to describe each problem. The constraint statement contains both a description of the difficulty and the reason for the problem. Listed below are some examples of constraint statements:

I don't know how to complete a resume because I never had any experience doing so.

I don't know what program is best for me because I have so many interests and can't make up my mind.

I can't find work right now because the plant has shut down and there is no work in my area.

Clients do not always give sufficient detail when describing their problems. One of the functions of the career counselor is to facilitate the exploration process so that a full description of the problem is obtained. The problem description is always done from the perspective of the client. Using one of the above examples, there might be some questions as to whether not finding a job is directly related to the plant shutting down. Nevertheless, that is how the client perceives the situation and the starting point is always the problem, as viewed through the eyes of the client.

There is not always just one simple problem to focus upon. There are often multiple problems that need to be assessed. It is not possible to do everything, and some choices have to be made. This is where the career counselor helps the client prioritize the issues that need to be addressed. It is usually better to focus on one or two issues and leave the rest until later. From a systems perspective, sometimes a positive change in one area can result in changes throughout the system (McMahon, 2005). For people who are unemployed, getting a job not only brings money into the home, it also can affect the nature of communication patterns in the home. Many problems disappear once the job situation is stabilized.

When considering the various problems that emerge, there may be some issues that fall outside of the expertise or mandate of the career counselor. The client isn't the only one making assessments about the problems that need to be resolved. Career counselors also need to be prepared to make referrals and to indicate which areas they would like to concentrate upon.

There are certain problem domains that typically fall within the career counseling mandate. Human Resources Development Canada refers to these areas as the employability dimensions and describes them as follows:

1. **Career Exploration and Decision Making**. People who have problems in this area are unsure about career options and may have difficulty in making decisions. These problems may relate to a lack of information about the labor market or be

reflective of a lack of self-knowledge about skills, values, interests, and personal style. Problems also can be associated with contextual variables such as the influence of family and friends.

2. **Occupational or Generic Skill Development.** People who have problems in this area lack the skill training to take advantage of work opportunities. Because of this need, they may need to consider training through colleges, universities, or training institutes. To succeed in our current society, in which life-long learning is a reality, people will need to move in and out of training throughout their career. Some of this training may occur in professional development contexts, and other training may require more formal educational study.

3. **Job Search Techniques.** The techniques for job search are culturally specific and do change over time. People who have been employed for long periods of time may find that they lack the skills required for a job search (the resume or portfolio, labor market analysis, calling employers, and interview skills). People who have entrepreneurial plans may need to learn how to establish and run a business.

4. **Job Maintenance Skills.** Many people are able to find work, but they have difficulty in keeping a job and being successful in their work. In the new work context, there are often fewer formal rules and some new requirements. Positive relationships with colleagues, customers, and supervisors must be established. There also is a need to learn strategies for career progression and development.

In addition to these general employability domains, there are other dimensions that can be added. At the beginning of the process, Borgen and Amundson (1996) have added the dimension of readiness to account for those people who are facing problems such as alcohol, drug abuse, and child care. Even though these other areas fall outside of the traditional employment counseling mandate, they do impact employment and can influence work choices and possibilities. Often, with these other domains, there is a need for community involvement and referral. Career counseling must be connected to other services within the broader community. An extra dimension can also be added after job maintenance. While there is certainly a need to maintain employment, for many people there are issues of enhancing employment skills and ongoing development. The notion of "growth" might be added to focus on some of the issues that apply within work itself.

People coming for career counseling often have problems that fall into more than one domain. The employability dimensions provide a road map of possibilities, and people can choose more than one area of concern. These problem areas have been described using the metaphor of a road map and are part of the Starting Points needs assessment program (Westwood, Amundson, & Borgen, 1994, p. 32). With the road map, there are roadblocks and stopovers (Figure 5.1). At the stopovers, people build resources for overcoming their problems. These resources can include courses, homework activities, training programs, and more.

To illustrate some of the components of the problem-defining process, consider the following example:

Background: Amanda is graduating from college with a double major in fine arts and computers. She is single, but has a boyfriend, and she is living at home with her parents. She is looking ahead to her career future.

FIGURE 5.1
The employment
roadmap

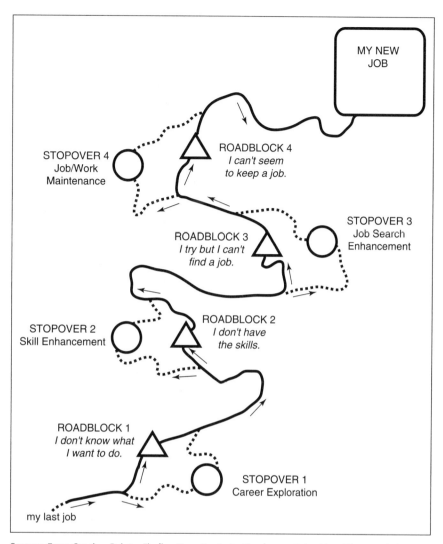

STOPOVER 4
Job/Work
Maintenance

ROADBLOCK 4
*I can't seem
to keep a job.*

MY NEW
JOB

STOPOVER 3
Job Search
Enhancement

ROADBLOCK 3
*I try but I can't
find a job.*

STOPOVER 2
Skill Enhancement

ROADBLOCK 2
*I don't have
the skills.*

ROADBLOCK 1
*I don't know what
I want to do.*

STOPOVER 1
Career Exploration

my last job

Source: From Starting Points: Finding Your Route to Employment, *by Marv Westwood, Norman Amundson, and William Borgen, Copyright © 1994, Human Resources Development Canada. This material is used by permission of Human Resources Development Canada.*

Amanda

A friend of mine told me that I should come to the center to discuss some of my career plans. I don't know what is really going to happen after graduation. I feel that I have been quietly paddling my canoe along the river but now realize that there is a bend in the river and some rapids lie ahead. I have been focusing on fine arts and computers but don't know where that is really heading. I don't know much

	about looking for work, I've always just had jobs handed to me. I am now working at a record company but I can't see that going anywhere. I have a boyfriend who is also graduating and talking about going traveling for a year. Is this a good idea? Maybe when I come back there won't be any jobs. Also, I don't know if I really have the funds to travel for a whole year.
Counselor	It sounds as if you have a lot going on in your life right now. Let's try to sort out some of the issues. As a starting point, you are graduating and you need to make some decisions about what jobs to pursue. Your concern is that you don't have enough experience with the labor market to know what types of positions might be available. A related problem is your lack of experience with a job search, even when you set your career direction you aren't sure that you have the job search skills to secure a position. And then there is the problem with your boyfriend and deciding whether to travel for a year. You are concerned about taking yourself out of the job market for a year and you have questions about funding for this length of time. Maybe you also aren't so sure whether this is something that you really want to do. Am I on track here with the issues that you are hoping to resolve?
Amanda	That's a pretty good summary; everything is so confusing right now.
Counselor	Hopefully, by sorting through some of the issues, we can cut through some of the confusion and attain greater clarity. Let's start by writing down the issues on this piece of paper (issues placed on paper—counselor checks to see that the list is complete).
Amanda	There are so many things to think about right now.
Counselor	It is overwhelming to try to tackle everything at the same time. As a starting point, think about what issue is the most pressing at this time. Perhaps we can rank the concerns.

(Note: The counselor might, at this point, choose to use the road map to illustrate some of the different possibilities. In this case, Amanda would likely be interested in pursuing career exploration and decision making as well as job search techniques.)

Amanda	Well, I guess the first thing to look at would be what kind of career to pursue after I graduate. Once I can get that clear I can think about this trip with my boyfriend.
Counselor	That sounds like a good choice Amanda, and it is certainly something that we can work on together.

ELABORATING THE PROBLEM

In this initial phase, there is often a need for further elaboration of the problem. There are many elements that could be explored for a fuller understanding of the situation. As a starting point, it is often helpful to get some further details about how the situation developed. Continuing with the preceding example, how did Amanda get interested in art and computers? Let's continue with the dialogue and see where it leads.

Counselor	Would you describe for me how your interests in art and computers first developed?
Amanda	Well, I always was interested in art and spent much of my free time doing freehand drawing. When it came time to go to college it seemed to be the best choice. Certainly, I enjoyed all my classes and think that I have really improved my artwork.
Counselor	That explains the art piece, how did you end up doing the double major in computers?
Amanda	My interest in computers came later when I thought about finding a job. I felt that I needed something that was more marketable—and everybody was talking about computers. I gave it a try and actually it seemed to go quite well.

(Upon this foundation, other questions can be asked. An obvious area for exploration includes significant relationships (family and friends). Returning to the dialogue:)

Counselor	Earlier, you mentioned that a friend advised you to come to the counseling center, and now you indicate that "everybody" was talking about computers, which influenced your career choice. What role do you see other people playing in your selection of a career direction?
Amanda	My parents and boyfriend are very supportive and basically let me decide what I want to do. I have a close girlfriend who is studying in the sciences, and she gives me a lot of good career advice. She told me that I never would get a job with just my art—and I think that she was right. You need to have a marketable skill, and I guess I was hoping that computers would be that employment ticket. Now, I'm not so sure. I started my program when there was a real "dot-com" mania, and I was hoping to ride along.

These additional questions add clarity and some new information. By focusing on relationships, the career counselor has learned about a close friend that seems to be playing a major role in the career choice process. This friend may need to be brought into the counseling process or at least acknowledged as the process unfolds. One important area that also emerged was the perceived relationship between art and computers. It is clear, from the dialogue, that there is very little connection being drawn between the two. Art is viewed as a personal interest, and computers are seen as a way to make a living. In terms of career planning, it seems that she has expended a minimal amount of effort. She was hoping to be part of the "dot-com" trend and to easily find work in the computer field. The changing economic climate has created a challenge that was unforeseen.

While a general picture of the situation is unfolding, there still is more specific information needed about what served as the "trigger" for her to come for career counseling (Amundson, 1995). Certainly, the "dot-com" problems have been escalating over the past few years, but what brought her to the point where she made the decision to come for counseling? Her friend plays a role here, and more details are needed. Continuing with the dialogue:

Counselor	The problems with "dot-com" firms have been growing during the past few years. What finally brought you to the point where you thought that you had better see a counselor?
Amanda	I don't like to think about the future, but it just seemed to get worse and worse. My girlfriend really started to get worried and she told me that I was going to need some help for this one. I finally decided to make an appointment, and here I am.

At this point it would be helpful to explore some of her expectations about career counseling. Given that Amanda was hoping to just ride the "dot-com" wave, is she now ready to put some time and energy toward career planning? There might be a need to discuss more fully what is required for effective career planning.

Counselor	What are you hoping to achieve in the time that we have together?
Amanda	My girlfriend mentioned that you had some tests that would show me some other career possibilities. I'm really stuck. My plan just hasn't worked out, but there must be something I can do.
Counselor	I wish there was a magic test that could solve all the problems, but it doesn't really work that way. It takes hard work and a willingness to review your own personal style and assets and also to explore the labor market. Are you prepared to commit to this type of process?

(Note: This is a good time to introduce the Wheel (see Figure 4.1) that was described in the previous chapter.)

VIEWING THE PROBLEM THROUGH A METAPHORIC LENS

The discussion, up to this point, has utilized a variety of exploratory questions and discussions. Another component is the visual imagery that often accompanies the telling of the story. Metaphors help us to visualize problems using a different framework, often one that is drawn from more familiar situations. The visual image reduces some of the fuzziness and confusion and helps to "pull things together." Visual imagery has the potential to reduce anxiety and increase a sense of creativity and self-efficacy (Combs & Freedman, 1990; Inkson & Amundson, 2002). In the story of Amanda, which we have been developing in this chapter, the following metaphor was incorporated into the telling of the story:

I feel that I have been quietly paddling my canoe along the river but now realize that there is a bend in the river and some rapids lie ahead.

This is an important element of the story and needs to be explored further. Let's continue with the dialogue:

Counselor	I was interested in the way in which you described your story, seeing yourself in a canoe and facing a change in direction and some rapids. Would you explain more about the image? Perhaps you could also draw it—how you saw it—on the flip chart.
Amanda	*(She constructs a drawing.)*
	This drawing really captures a number of different emotions. On the one hand, there is the tranquility of the last few years. I have been enjoying classes and have not been thinking too much about the future. It has just been one step in front of the other—in this case I guess it would be the constant rowing motion. And then there is the unknown coming up, suddenly I will be going a new direction and the rapids present a totally new challenge. It is a lot to take in at one time.
Counselor	Looking at your drawing I am struck by how tranquil everything appears now, and then there is the giant problem looming ahead. Has the water always been that tranquil for you?
Amanda	I guess that is what it's been like for the past two years, but before that there were a lot of challenges. I had some difficulties making the transition from high school to college and I'm glad that that time is behind me.
Counselor	So you've already come through a set of rapids. Now you are facing another challenge.

(Note: By drawing attention to past accomplishments, you draw attention to Amanda's ability to overcome challenges.)

Amanda	That's an interesting way to put it. Yes, I guess that I have gone through some rapids before.
Counselor	In your drawing, you only have yourself in the canoe moving forward. How do your friends and family fit into this picture? (Note: discussed further in Chapter 7)
Amanda	Well, my boyfriend would be way out front wanting me to catch up and go off in another direction. And my girlfriend

would be paddling beside me, helping me keep going. Let me make a change to the drawing; actually what is coming up is a split in the river—with one part going over some rapids and another part heading off in a new direction—that's where you will find my boyfriend.

(The client makes a change to the drawing.)

Counselor	You haven't included me in your drawing. How do you see my role in all of this?
Amanda	Well, you would be on the other side of the canoe (client adds a new figure to the drawing), coaching me through the rough parts that lie ahead.

The elaboration of the metaphor has brought forward some new information about perceived challenges and past accomplishments. It also is interesting to see how the different people align themselves with respect to the problem. As with the earlier elaboration, questions regarding development over time and the involvement of others help to provide a broader perspective on the problem. By including the career counselor in the drawing, there also is a focus on the perceived role of the career counselor.

Using this format, the career counselor can respond to the problem and to role expectations by adding or changing parts of the image. Rather than just talking about issues, the counselor can work to adjust the perceived image. It should be noted here that in the case illustration there was an easy access to a flip chart. By having this resource close at hand the counselor was able to include drawings as part of the process with minimal interruption. If one wants to work in this medium, then it is important to have the necessary tools close at hand.

Of course, not all clients may be willing to construct drawings of their metaphors. While drawings are helpful, they are not essential to the use of this technique. Sometimes it is enough to simply talk about the image, without having an actual drawing. In other cases, the career counselor might want to do the drawing. And if the person (client or counselor) just doesn't seem to work well in this modality, it is then set aside and other approaches are used. There is nothing magical about metaphors, but they can be a useful career counseling resource. Many people do have a strong visual orientation but don't get the opportunity to fully utilize this capacity in the career counseling situation.

CHANGING DIRECTION

The identified problem is a good starting point for career counseling, but as the discussion proceeds other problems might emerge. Even though some work has been done at the beginning to identify the problem, it is not uncommon to have a change in direction as the discussion proceeds. This change in focus may be a new awareness for the client, or it might be the result of increased trust in the counselor. Let's continue with the earlier dialogue and see how changes might develop.

Counselor	It looks, from this drawing, that you are moving toward the rapids but you still have this other pull by your boyfriend toward the new direction.
Amanda	Yeh, that's it. I don't know how to tell him that I don't want to go with him. I feel that I will really hurt his feelings if I don't go with him. The pressure is just so terrible.
Counselor	It sounds as if we really have two problems emerging. On one hand there is the upcoming rapids but, on the other, there is the issue of how to talk with your boyfriend about your wishes.
Amanda	Yes, that's what I really have to do right now—I need to talk more about my relationship with him. I can't really think about this other stuff until I figure out our relationship.
Counselor	Maybe I can help you explore some aspects of your relationship and then we can come back to the issue of the fast-approaching rapids.

This discussion illustrates some of the overlap between career and personal counseling. At this point, the counselor has agreed to spend some time discussing Amanda's relationship with her boyfriend. Of course, if this discussion about the boyfriend were to progress into other personal areas that were beyond the skill level of the counselor, it would be important to consider making a referral.

Throughout the career counseling process, the counselor must be flexible and ready to return to the problem definition if this is warranted. The career counseling process is not linear. It can be helpful to check at various points to ensure that "the problem" is still "the problem."

SUMMARY

An important step in the career counseling process is the specification of the problem. People often come to counseling with a multitude of personal, as well as career, issues. Rather than trying to do too much, the career counselor must help the client focus on one issue at a time. Prioritizing and selecting issues becomes the first task in the career counseling process.

Once an appropriate career issue has been agreed upon, there is a need to get further information about the problem. Questions concerning how the problem developed and the people involved (context) serve as a good beginning. These questions can be raised directly or as part of a metaphoric inquiry. With metaphors, there also is the option of using drawings to illustrate various facets of the problem.

As more information is gathered, there are times when a problem may start to change. In these instances, the career counselor needs to be flexible and seek clarification about the problem that is being pursued. Career counseling is not a linear process, and in some circumstances, there can be significant changes in the problem under discussion. Career counselors must be prepared to change direction when warranted and also must be sensitive to the need to make referrals if the situation extends beyond mandate and personal competence levels.

CHAPTER 6

Exploring the Problem: Understanding the Self

- **Questioning and Storytelling**
- **Metaphors**
- **Structured Assessment**
- **Limitations**

Once the relationship has been established and the problem identified, there is room for further exploration. As was indicated in Chapter 2, this exploration often focuses on the individual (understanding oneself better) and the context (understanding the contextual and labor market options). The length of time for this exploration varies considerably. With this exploration, there is the expectation that the client is working collaboratively with the career counselor and doing some exploratory work (homework activities) outside the counseling sessions. In this chapter, we will focus on self-understanding and will be examining some of the ways in which self-exploration might proceed.

As people try to establish a career direction it is important that they have some understanding of their skills, interests, values, and personal style. Referring back to the wheel diagram (see Figure 4.1) these personal skills and attributes are represented on the bottom half of the wheel. A major focus in career counseling is the exploration of these segments of the wheel and the organization of this information into a coherent whole. There are many different ways of undertaking this exploratory process. The exploration can proceed with further questioning and storytelling, metaphors, and the completion of standardized and nonstandardized inventories.

QUESTIONING AND STORYTELLING

1. IN SEARCH OF FLOW AND EXCELLENCE (SELF)

This first theme emphasizes excellence and the joy found when one is involved with activities for which one feels a sense of passion and commitment. There may be some sense of achievement involved and also a sense of what Csikszentmihalyi (1990) describes as "flow." These experiences can come from any aspect of working or personal life. Some typical questions that fit within this thematic area are as follows:

- Describe a personally rewarding accomplishment from any part of your life.
- What subjects did you enjoy in school?
- What hobbies or outside interests do you have?
- Describe some absorbing childhood activities.
- Describe a situation where you really felt energized.

We have found with some of these questions that it also can be helpful to look at the negative counterpart. So, for example, the counselor could ask about subjects that the person doesn't enjoy, as well as those that are favorites. Sometimes, these more negative examples can also provide some new insights.

When responding to these types of questions, some people will provide elaborate answers and others will give shorter answers. It is important to follow with supplemental questions that expand the information that is provided. Sometimes, real understanding only comes when you look at the details. For example, if someone says that he enjoys science class, ask for more information about what makes science class so special. For some people it might be specific types of content, for others it might be the people in the class or the instructor; perhaps it is the type of lab assignments that were included. Whatever the case, give the person an opportunity to elaborate on his initial answer.

One specific illustration of this type of exploration is the Pattern Identification Exercise (Amundson, 2003). With this exercise, the starting point is the identification of an interest area and specific descriptions of times when it went well and when it was more challenging. Let's use a case illustration to describe the process.

Background: James is in his mid-twenties and has drifted through a number of different jobs. He has a bachelor of arts degree but no real career direction. Recently, he was working as a salesperson in a car dealership and was let go because of poor sales.

Counseling Process

James obviously had some good social skills and it was relatively easy to establish rapport. He identified a lack of career direction as his main career counseling issue. As part of the exploration process he completed the Pattern Identification Exercise. When asked about an area of interest, he identified tennis as something that he really enjoyed. What follows is some of the dialogue:

Counselor	What I would like you to do is to think of a specific time with tennis when it was really enjoyable for you, as well as a time when maybe it didn't go so well.
James	Well I really enjoy tennis for the exercise and for the fellowship.
Counselor	I want you to get concrete here and think about a specific time when it went well and when it didn't. Can you think of something?
	(Pause.)
James	OK.

(Note: It is important to insist on specific examples, sometimes people give answers that are too general.)

Counselor	You can start with either the positive or the negative example. Is it OK if I just write down on this flip chart what you are saying so that we can keep track of the information?
James	Yes, that's OK. Let's start with the positive situation.

(Note: What follows is a summary of the description, in list form, as written down by the career counselor—using the words of the client.)

Positive—Playing Tennis

- Playing in a tournament with one of the better players.
- My game was really on.
- I was hitting my backhand with authority and placing the shots.
- My mind was really working overtime.

- I really felt in control of my game.
- He was also hitting some good shots, and I was really being challenged.
- Even though I didn't win, I felt satisfied with how I had performed and what I had learned.

Negative—Playing Tennis
- Playing in the same tournament with another opponent.
- This time I just couldn't seem to do anything right.
- He wasn't taking me seriously.
- All he had was a big serve but that was enough to put me away.

Counselor	When you look at this information, do you see any patterns?
James	Well, I guess it says that I like to perform well and to be taken seriously. I like to be challenged but also to be learning something new. It doesn't really matter whether I win or lose as long as I am learning something.
Counselor	You mentioned, in your description, that you like to be in control. Can you say more about this?
James	I really like to be mentally stimulated and to focus on getting the small details right. I like to hit the ball well and to place it just where I want it to be.
Counselor	So it's not so much about winning or losing, but "how you play the game."
James	Yes, that's the important part for me.

Following this dialogue, the discussion shifted to a consideration of how these patterns fit with his current situation and where he would like to go in the future. What stood out was his love of learning, his need for mental stimulation, and his need to be fully involved in each situation. In the car dealership he was bored and had difficulty "closing the sale." He wanted to make sure that his customers saw all the options, but he sometimes moved too slowly and didn't close the deal. As the counselor explored his situation further, James came to the conclusion that what he really wanted was to pursue a career in adult education. As an adult educator, he would be able to work with people who would stimulate his own learning. From the negative example, he realized that some of his earlier frustration with postsecondary schooling was the result of instructors not taking him seriously. When this happened he found himself reacting in ways that interfered with his own learning. Some of the learning in career counseling revolved around ways to ensure that he could "play his game" regardless of the situation.

You will notice, in following this example, that the role of the career counselor during this exercise is primarily one of facilitation. The client describes the situation and the counselor ensures that a full description is recorded. In the analysis phase, the client makes some preliminary observations. The counselor can offer some further questions and tentative observations, but the primary focus is always on the analysis by the client. There will be some situations in which the counselor may need to take a more active role. However, for the most part, the counselor should let the client do as much of their own analysis and application as possible.

2. IN SEARCH OF FLOW AND EXCELLENCE (OTHERS)

This second segment is really a subset of the first section. Rather than examining personal achievements and attributes, there is a focus on the admirable qualities and actions of others. We tend to appreciate people who express qualities and strengths that we value for ourselves. The following questions reflect this approach:

- List some people that you admire and describe what it is about them that you find admirable.
- When you think about the books you have read, what characters do you find admirable and what is it that they do?

Once admirable characters have been identified, the focus shifts to what this admiration means in terms of values, interests, personality, and strengths. The qualities that we admire in others often have some meaning for our own lives. For example, suppose that your client, Emily, indicated that Mother Theresa was someone that she really admired. In exploring further she might indicate that she really admired Mother Theresa's courage, her compassion and her dedication in the fact of some very real challenges. From this point you might proceed in several directions. One possibility would be to ask Emily about the challenges she has faced in her life and examine how some of the qualities of Mother Theresa were a part of the way in which she handled difficult situations. Perhaps there is also something here that Emily can draw upon as she faces her current problems.

Another way to consider relationships with others is to focus on how a person would like to be seen by others. What type of legacy is being created and looking ahead, how would the person like to be remembered? By viewing our relationship with others in this way we can investigate the past, the present, and the future. Contained within the legacy concept of legacy is the notion that our actions have a direct influence on how we are viewed at the present time and also how we would like to be viewed.

3. NO WORRIES, MATE

The Australians use the phrase "no worries mate" to indicate that all is well. Applying this to career counseling, you can consider how life would look if all our problems were set aside. Perhaps there are financial details to worry about or the reactions of other people (such as parents or friends). Whatever the circumstances, it can be helpful to dream a little and imagine what would happen without the usual restraints. Some questions that fit within this framework are as follows:

- How would your life change if you won a large sum of money?
- What would you do if you didn't have to worry about what other people thought or said?
- If you could have any job you wanted, what would you choose?
- Imagine that your problem is solved (don't worry about the details); what would your solution look like?

The last question in the list of questions is used by solution-focused counselors (De Shazer, 1985; O'Hanlon & Weiner-Davis, 1989; Friedman, 1993) as part of a counseling technique called the "miracle question." People are told to imagine that a miracle has occurred and that their problem is solved. They then are instructed to look back at the problem from the place of solution. Usually we start with the problem and move towards a solution. In this case, the process is reversed. When using this technique, you can also have clients physically move to another side of the room or the hallway to represent the change in position. Starting from the solution gives people better perspective and is more empowering. The change in perspective also can help provide a reality check. As people look back at what needs to be done, they may decide that they aren't standing in the right place.

Dreams can change over time and another option would be to explore a "dream line." What were some of the first ideas about work possibilities and how did these change with the passage of time? Also, what accounted for some of these changes, was it other people, circumstances, or something else? And finally, if you look into the future what are some other dreams that might develop? Exploring dreams in this way helps to increase self-understanding and to open up new possibilities.

4. STRENGTHS IN OTHER PLACES

Often, when clients are describing their problems, they are so focused on what they can't do that they lose sight of what is working and how they have solved problems in other situations. What can be helpful is to shift perspective so that they can see some other strengths. Listed below are some questions that support this change in perspective.

- We have spent considerable time discussing what didn't go well (for example, being unable to do well in an interview). I would also like you to describe some times when you did respond appropriately.
- This isn't the first time you have faced problems in your life. I would like to hear about some of the times when you were able to overcome challenges and reach a positive solution. (Note: An example of this type of question was used in Chapter 5 when Amanda talked about successfully going through a set of rapids prior to finding the calmer water.)

By using these type of questions, clients are encouraged to view problems from a more balanced and positive perspective. Rather than focus exclusively on the negative, they are asked to consider times when things were going well. They are also encouraged to think about other problem situations when they have been successful. The problem-solving skills that they previously used can be applied to new situations.

METAPHORS

Chapter 5 suggested that metaphors are a useful way of understanding problems. One can also use metaphoric language to help change perspectives on problems. To illustrate this process we will continue the dialogue with Amanda (from Chapter 5).

Background: Amanda has redrawn the figure so that she is in the middle with her friend on one side and the career counselor on the other. She is heading toward the rapids. Her boyfriend is off to the side, wanting her to go in another direction, but she is ignoring him (for the moment). She has already been through a set of rapids but the water is now calm.

Counselor	I would like to hear more about your earlier experience with the rapids.
Amanda	It was really rough for a while. I didn't have any friends and it was a totally new situation. But I hung in there and did my best, and eventually I met some people and began to understand the system.
Counselor	I guess one of the defining characteristics of being in the rapids is that you don't have a lot of other people travelling alongside. It's quite a different experience from what you are experiencing now (pointing to the drawing).
Amanda	That's interesting. Yeah, I guess when it all changes I won't have you and Denise at my side like I do now. I'll have to be ready to handle things on my own.
Counselor	You managed fine with the last set of rapids.
Amanda	Yeah, I guess I did, but these are more daunting.
Counselor	Let's work with this image and brainstorm some other options. How can you change the drawing to give you more power?

Result of Brainstorming
- Bigger boat.
- Find another way around the rapids.
- Learn some new skills.
- Learn more about the rapids and what lies ahead.

Counselor	Those look like some interesting ideas, let's see how we can apply some of these ideas to your situation.

In this scenario, the counselor stayed with the client's image and focused the problem solving through a brainstorming activity. From this foundation, further discussion can develop around using transferable skills (from the previous experience), learning more about the current context, and developing new skills.

Another way to proceed with metaphors is to help the client develop other metaphors for the situation. Combs and Freedman (1990, p. 32) make the case that creativity and flexibility are enhanced through the creation of multiple metaphors.

Any single metaphor is a particular version of a particular part of the world. When people have only one metaphor for a situation, their creativity is limited. The more metaphors they have to choose from for a given situation the more choice and flexibility they have in how to handle it. Finding multiple metaphors expands the realm of creativity.

There are a number of different ways of looking at career metaphors. Inkson (2007) and Inkson and Amundson (2002) describe a number of possibilities some of which are listed below:

1. **The journey:** Viewing career as movement on a career path toward a destination.
2. **An inheritance:** Career involvement is something that is passed on intergenerationally; such as the family farm or business.
3. **Fit:** The work world and the person are viewed as having particular shapes, and the focus is on deriving a match (fitting square pegs into square holes).
4. **Seasons or Cycles:** Career as a series of definable stages (seasons of life).
5. **Growth:** Viewing career as something organic, where there is ongoing development and learning.
6. **Creative work:** Career as something that has been designed or crafted, a work of art.
7. **Network:** From a collective perspective, career is viewed as being closely aligned to group norms and expectations.
8. **Resource:** Career, from this perspective, uses a term such as "human resource management" to reflect the linkages to the economy and to planning initiatives.
9. **Story:** With this focus, the emphasis is on the narrative and creating meaning in our lives through stories.
10. **Cultural artifact:** Viewing career as a reflection of our cultural contexts.

These metaphoric images capture a variety of different perspectives on career. In Amanda's case, she is following a "journey" metaphor but one could also look at her situation in terms of "growth." From this perspective, change is natural and nothing to be feared or avoided. For example, if one uses the image of the caterpillar in the cocoon, change is an exciting process of new development. During the process, wings are acquired and the world is explored with increased energy and possibility.

With both metaphors and questioning, there is a dynamic quality. The career counselor must be prepared to use intuition and follow the story as it evolves. Questions and metaphors serve as probes for exploration and serve to stimulate the client's storytelling. In the next section more structure is introduced and the focus of exploration becomes more defined.

STRUCTURED ASSESSMENT

There are many different forms of structured assessment. Perhaps the most common form is a situation in which clients respond to a standard set of questions that tap into some broader dimensions. The advantage of using a standard set of questions is that some comparisons can be made with other people. Of course, this form of assessment also requires some special training—particularly for the interpretation of results. To appreciate the full range of assessment possibilities and the issues related to reliability and validity, one needs to take a specific course on this topic or make a referral to a trained career counseling professional.

Niles and Harris-Bowlsbey (2002) suggest that there are three different purposes for assessment. The first form of assessment focuses on client needs such as career maturity, irrational beliefs, or decision-making ability. Listed below are some common formal assessment tools that fall into this category:

- **Career Maturity Inventory (CMI).** Examines the readiness of students to make career decisions. A measure appropriate for students in grades 6–12 (Crites & Savickas, 1995).
- **Career Thoughts Inventory (CTI).** Identifies the irrational thoughts that might hinder people when making career decisions. A measure appropriate for high school students and adults (Sampson, Peterson, Lenz, Reardon, & Saunders, 1996).
- **Career Development Inventory (CDI).** An inventory designed to assess readiness for career decision-making. A measure appropriate for high school and college students (Super, Thompson, Lindeman, Jordan, & Myers, 1984).
- **Career Decision Scale (CDS).** A scale designed to assess how indecisiveness prevents people from making good career decisions. A measure appropriate for high school students and adults (Osipow, Carney, Winer, Yanico, & Koschier, 1997).
- **The Career Beliefs Inventory.** An inventory that examines the problematic self-perceptions and world views that hinder career decision-making. A measure appropriate for high school students and adults (Krumboltz, 1991).

These inventories focus on some of the issues that support or hinder a client's career development process.

The other purposes for assessment are to help clients and the career counselor know more about the self and to provide a mechanism for measuring progress or change. Some common measures with this focus are as follows:

- **Self-Directed Search (SDS).** An inventory that assesses personality type and interest for six different occupational groups. This measure can be self-administered, self-scored, and self-interpreted; and it can be used with high school students, college students, and adults. (Holland, 1994).
- **The Strong Interest Inventory (SII).** This broadly based inventory uses Holland types (RIASEC) and provides basic interest scales, general interest scales, general occupational themes, as well as administrative indices and special scales such as introversion–extroversion. This framework provides comparisons between the examinee's profile and that of workers in many different occupations. This measure is best suited for senior adolescents and adults. (Campbell, Strong, & Hansen, 1991).
- **Jackson Vocational Interest Survey (JVIS).** An educational and career planning interest survey (34 scales). This measure is appropriate for high school students, college students, and adults. (Jackson, 1991).
- **Harrington-O'Shea Career Decision Making System (CDMS).** A career interest and decision-making system that uses a structure similar to the Holland codes. The CDMS is appropriate for high school students and adults. (Harrington & O'Shea, 1992).
- **Kuder Career Search with Person Match (Kuder).** Measures interests in ten categories of activities and six occupational clusters. There also is a database

that examinees can use to compare their results and gather information about the occupations that are most similar to their profile. This measure is appropriate for high school students, college students, and adults. (Zytowski & Kuder, 1999).

- **Career Occupational Preference Survey (COPS).** A survey that assesses interests in eight career clusters, five of which can be divided into professional and skilled levels. This measure is appropriate for students in grades seven to twelve, for college students, and for adults. (Knapp & Knapp, 1992).
- **The Career Planning Survey (CPS).** A survey that assesses abilities and interests. The Holland interest types are used, and these are linked to the World-of-Work Map. This measure is appropriate for high school students, college students, and adults. (ACT, 1997).
- **The General Aptitude Test Battery (GATB).** Measures nine vocational aptitudes and can be used in conjunction with the U.S. Employment Service interest inventory. This measure is appropriate for high school students, college students, and adults. (U.S. Employment Service, 1982)
- **The Myers–Briggs Type Indicator (MBTI).** This personality assessment measure is based on Carl Jung's types and provides a score based on four scales. The results can be related to typical profiles of people working in specific occupations as well as serving as a focus for facilitating better communication in work teams. This measure is appropriate for high school students, college students, and adults. (Myers & Briggs, 1993).

These assessment measures focus on personal characteristics and provide people with information so that they can compare their personal qualities and skills with occupational environments.

In addition to the assessment measures listed above, there are many online assessment tools (such as DISCOVER and SIGI) that need to be considered. These approaches are discussed in Chapter 8 as part of a broader discussion on the use of websites in career counseling.

There are also some structured inventories that are more exploratory in their focus. The process is similar in that clients respond to a prescribed set of questions. What differs is that the responses are interpreted loosely, without any specific comparative analysis. These inventories do not usually require the same level of assessment background and training.

Another form of structured assessment is the card sort. With a card sort, items are often placed on index cards and are then sorted in different ways (Gysbers & Moore, 1987). For example, one might list a series of values on cards and then ask clients to choose those values that have the best fit. The same could be done with lists of interests, personal qualities, skills, work-place characteristics, or job options. There are usually three groupings; those that fit very well, those that definitely do not match, and those where there is some level of indecision. In some cases, this is followed by further refinement as people are asked to rank order the cards for which there was the highest level of fit.

There are many different types of card sorts. Some are individually constructed by counselors, and others are purchased from people who have specialized in this form of product development. With some card sorts, such as the Intelligent Career Card Sort (see website www.intelligentcareer.net), there is the provision of special training in the same way as with other assessment instruments. The ICCS includes some additional career exploration processes and also provides an opportunity for comparative analysis.

LIMITATIONS

As was mentioned in Chapter 1, many clients come to career counseling expecting that there is a powerful test that they can take that will tell them exactly what career direction they should pursue. No such testing instrument exists—or could exist given our dynamic and changing society. Structured assessment methods have an important role to play in the exploration process, but their limitations should be realized. This is why it is so important to have the proper training when assessing and using these instruments.

Another issue that must be considered when facilitating career exploration is the applicability of certain measures in diverse counseling contexts (culture, race, gender, socioeconomic status, or age). With open-ended questioning and storytelling, there is room for individual differences to emerge. The same can be said for the use of metaphors. These methods lend themselves to an open and nonjudgmental process. With the more structured techniques, more caution needs to be applied. If comparisons are being made, there is a need to examine the types of people who were used to develop norms for the tests. Also, the relevance and applicability of certain test items might need to be evaluated. While there certainly can be some advantages to deriving comparisons, this information is only as useful as the foundation upon which it rests.

SUMMARY

This chapter has emphasized exploration efforts that focus specifically on the self. There are myriad ways that this can occur. We have highlighted some questions that can be used to further this process. These questions can focus on personal strengths and achievements and times when there seems to be a general sense of "flow." These positive moments can either be directly related to the problem or come from other related areas in a person's life. Positive moments can also address some of the strengths we see and admire in others. Another approach is to use imagination and visualization to help people move past barriers to the end goals. From this new perspective, there is an opportunity to reassess problems and career directions.

Metaphors were also explored as a means for creating new perspectives on problems. With this approach, there is an attempt to adjust and change metaphors to create new images. Having multiple metaphors is useful to build creativity and flexibility. As people learn to change perspectives, their ability to solve problems and generate new options increases.

The final career exploration section focuses on more structured methods of assessment. These inventories are useful for examining personal characteristics and abilities. They also can be applied to other areas such as the assessment of career maturity, irrational beliefs, and decision-making ability. While most structured assessment uses a traditional inventory structure there also are other ways to organize the information. Card sorts, for example, are one way to include more visual and kinesthetic components into the counseling process.

When using career exploration methods there also are some limitations that must be acknowledged. Clients often expect too much from the use of traditional tests, and this expectation requires some clarification. Career counselors must be aware of the normative structure of the tests they are using and must apply them appropriately. Issues of diversity are particularly important when making comparisons.

The next chapter continues the focus on exploration but moves from the individual to the broader social and cultural context, including the dynamics of the labor market. Career development needs to be driven by an understanding of the individual and by an appreciation of these broader contextual issues.

7

Exploring the Problem: Contextual and Labor Market Options

- **Social Context**
- **Educational and Work/Leisure Context**
- **Labor Market Options (A Personal View)**

Once a sense of self-understanding is attained, there is a need to focus on the broader contextual factors and labor market options (see Chapters 3 and 6). These factors are represented in Super's archway and in the upper half of the Career Wheel that was described in Chapter 4. We always live in conversation with our world and need to adopt a holistic perspective where both the self and the external world are considered together.

SOCIAL CONTEXT

Within North America, we often minimize the importance of the social context and overemphasize the importance of the self. In many other cultures there is a different balance between internal (the self) and external factors, with greater significance being attached to group identity (Hampden-Turner & Trompenaars, 2000; Hofstede, 1997; McCormick & Amundson, 1997). In career counseling we need to take account of both the individual and the group identity.

As an illustration of how we might need to make some adjustments to our traditional career counseling methods, consider the questions being asked by Cooper (2001) in his popular book *The Other 90%*. He makes the case that most people only use a small portion of their talents and abilities. To help people broaden their perspectives, he asks the following two questions:

1. What's the most exceptional thing you've done this week?
2. What's the most exceptional thing you will do next week? (p. 8)

The word "exceptional" is loosely defined and can refer to any way in which you did something special over the week. It doesn't have to be a momentous event, simply something that stands out for you. Before going further, take a moment and reflect on these questions.

The idea of focusing attention on some of our "exceptional" moments is not a new one and fits nicely with some of the exercises that were outlined in Chapter 6. This perspective has a very strong emphasis on the actions of the self. What would happen if we changed these questions and gave them a stronger group focus? The questions would become

1. What's the most exceptional thing you have done this week as part of a group?
2. What's the most exceptional thing you will do next week as part of a group?

Try answering these additional questions and notice how your perspective changes. Rather than thinking "I was special" the focus shifts to being part of a team. This is what is meant by the "group identity." Clients may put different emphasis on the two sets of questions, but we believe that both sets of questions need to be asked.

Given the importance, for many people, of the social group, we must ask some questions about the significance that other people hold for them in their career planning. This can be done in a structured format by having people make a list of the people who are close to them (perhaps grouping the people according to their level of closeness), including family members and other friendship networks. Once a comprehensive list has been made, then have people add in what types of careers these people have had, in what ways have they provided support, and also any career advice that they might have offered. This information can be used as a vehicle for further career discussion. For example, what types of career support are being given? Support can come in many different forms. For some, it may involve tangible resources such as money or goods, others will offer informational support, and there is also emotional support. These different forms of support can overlap with one another and also can change over time. And then there is the issue of career advice. As they consider the advice that has been offered, what has been their response to this advice? These reactions can become significant "drivers" in the career journey.

Incorporating information from significant others can be done in many different ways. In addition to some questions about social context, it is possible to seek out some direct input by using the Significant Other Questionnaire (Amundson, 2003, p. 196). This questionnaire includes the following instructions and questions:

Please complete the following questions. Your opinion is important to help _____ make future career plans; therefore, your honesty is greatly appreciated.

1. What would you say this person is good at? What skills has this person demonstrated?

2. What would you see as this person's major interest areas?

3. How would you describe the personal characteristics of this person?

4. What positive changes have you noticed over time in this person, especially in relation to work or looking for work?

5. In what ways could this person continue to improve?

6. What positive skills and attributes have you noticed about this person that might go unrecognized?

7. If you were to suggest the ideal job or career prospect for this person, what would it be?[1]

There must be an initial discussion about who would be the best person to complete the form. There also is a need for some debriefing after the information has been gathered.

Let's consider again the case of Amanda. The key players in her situation would be Denise (friend), her boyfriend, and her parents. The dialogue might develop as follows:

Counselor   There are a number of people who seem to have ideas about your career future: Denise, your boyfriend, and your parents. Would you be interested in using this questionnaire to gather some additional information?

[1]From *Active Engagement*. Amundson, N., p. 196, 2003, Ergon Communications.

Amanda	That would be fine. I would like to give it to Denise and my boyfriend, but I can't see any point in giving it to my parents. They never say anything about what I should do.
Counselor	The other side of the argument is that this questionnaire does provide a framework for giving some input.
Amanda	Yeah, I guess it wouldn't hurt to give them all a copy.

Later

Counselor	I see that you have the Significant Other Questionnaires with you today.
Amanda	Yes, everybody responded right away. I felt a little strange asking them to do this, but it has been an interesting exercise.
Counselor	What things have you learned?
Amanda	I knew pretty well what Denise and my boyfriend were going to say, but it still felt good seeing it on paper. They really have a lot of faith in me. What surprised me was what my parents put down. Somehow they got the idea that they shouldn't interfere, but they had lots of good things to say.
Counselor	It might be worthwhile to spend some time looking at all this information.
Amanda	I would like that.

The questionnaire has the potential to add some new information. It is a structured way to examine the perspectives of other people and also their suggestions for future directions.

A more direct way to involve significant others is to invite them, with approval from the client, to one of the career counseling sessions. If there is approval from the client, invite people to one of the career counseling sessions. Chances are that they are going to talk about the session anyway, so you might as well deal with them directly. They don't have to be at every session, but this is one possibility.

In situations where parents are invited to career counseling sessions, it might be advisable to use an approach whereby parents are primarily put in the role of observers (Amundson & Penner, 1998). Otherwise, there is the risk of having parents take over the counseling session. This doesn't mean that they don't have an opportunity to provide some input. The main point is that there is some formal structure to ensure that a young person does not get overwhelmed by the presence of parents.

When a significant other is more involved in the career counseling process, she is able to provide important contextual information. There also is greater opportunity to view some of the ways in which she interacts with the client.

EDUCATIONAL AND WORK/LEISURE CONTEXT

As people seek to find a place for themselves in the career marketplace, they must make reference to their education and work/leisure experiences. These variables play an important role in defining the career opportunities that will be available. For example, with Amanda, she has a degree with a double major in fine arts and computers. This educational background will define the opportunities that are available to her.

We have found that many people have some understanding of how their education and work/leisure experiences connect with the labor market, but this understanding is often rather limited. Let's return to Amanda's situation to see how this understanding might be broadened.

Counselor	You've told me that you have a double major in fine arts and computers. How were you hoping to use this education in your work search?
Amanda	Well, I don't think that fine arts will be of much help, but I was hoping to do some work with computers. Unfortunately, everything has really taken a downturn.
Counselor	I wonder if you might not be taking full advantage of your education? Are there any ways of combining your fine arts with computers?
Amanda	They are really completely different worlds. I can't see much of a fit.
Counselor	Maybe there is something that you are overlooking. Why don't you spend some time in the career library seeing if there are any ways that you can put the two together? The career librarian will help you sort through some of the job catalogues.

Later

Amanda	I think I've come up with something. I found this career called graphic design. People seem to work with computers, but they also are using their creativity to come up with interesting images.
Counselor	If you want to learn more about graphic design, it might be helpful to do an information interview.
Amanda	What's an information interview?
Counselor	With this type of interview, you find people who are actually working in the area. You aren't asking them for a job, just an opportunity to meet with them for a short while to discuss how they view their jobs. Perhaps we could brainstorm how to connect with these people and also determine what questions you might ask.

In Amanda's situation there was a need to link fine arts and computers. With other people, some other form of expansion might be necessary. In one situation, we were working with a client who had nursing training but wanted to expand her horizons (Amundson & Poehnell, 1996). In this situation, we put the word "nurse" in the center of the page and then brainstormed some other options. Listed below are some of the connections that were made:

nutritionist
dental hygienist
midwife

dietician
radiologist
medical lab technician
pharmacy aide
medical claims assessor
nursing instructor
occupational health

This form of expansion helps people to see how their skills can be transferred into other areas. They may need some additional training, but their education can be applied to new situations.

Expanding horizons is something that also applies to work and leisure experiences. People often underestimate the skills that they have acquired. This is particularly the case with newly arrived immigrants and with women returning to work. In these situations, and with others, there may be an inability to see the full range of skills imbedded within the experiences. Clients facing this barrier need to be challenged to develop a greater appreciation of their transferable skills. Career counselors can play a key role in helping clients make the connections between their experiences and the labor market. One tool that can be helpful in this regard is the list of skills, attitudes, and behaviors developed by the Conference Board of Canada (http://www.conferenceboard.ca/nbec). This list was developed with input from employers and focuses on the employability skills needed for success in the workplace. Employability skills include the following:

- communication skills
- problem-solving skills
- positive attitudes and behaviors
- adaptability
- working with others
- science, technology, and mathematical skills

When clients see this list, they often become more aware of how their previous experience might be applied in a new context.

In addition to expanding horizons, it can also be important to explore, in detail, the various aspects of education and work/leisure experience. To give an example, one client was working as an accountant and decided that she needed a change. She was frustrated in her job and wanted to explore other career options. As the career counselor helped her to explore her frustrations at work, there was the realization that some aspects of the social situation might be having an influence. She was working at a job where she traveled to a number of different offices during the course of a week. She had difficulty forming relationships and usually spent her lunch hours and breaks sitting by herself. Further exploration revealed that she really did enjoy accounting; the main problem was the lack of relationships at work. With this new understanding, she looked for a new job where she could stay in one office. She found another job, and in this new context her dissatisfaction disappeared. What was needed was a change in workplace—not a change in career.

LABOR MARKET OPTIONS (A PERSONAL VIEW)

There are many different ways of looking at the labor market. Many clients come to career counseling searching for a guarantee for the future. They want to know what they can take that will ensure them a job at the end of their training. There certainly are some general trends that can be discussed (Herr, 1999; Storey, 2000) and these include:

1. need for higher levels of educational training
2. globalization (multinational corporations)
3. increased use of communication and information technology
4. privatization of the public sector
5. demographic and labor market changes (changes in age, gender, and ethnic composition)
6. changing organizational forms and structures (less middle management; downsizing)
7. more flexible employment patterns (temporary and part-time work, flex time, self-employment)
8. changing values (focus on life/work balance, environmental concerns, dual career families)
9. changing the implicit psychological contract (less loyalty to the organization, more project-based work arrangements)
10. increased job insecurity (less reliance on tenure and seniority, more contractual work, periods of unemployment)

While these trends provide some general guidelines, they are only one part of a broader employment picture. In addition to general guidelines, people need to be aware of their own particular interests and skills and their own "personal labor market." One's "personal labor market" refers to the opportunities and options that exist because of personal connections and actions.

Many people fail to identify and to fully expand and utilize their personal labor market. They fail to recognize all the people who could be a part of their personal network. Sometimes, all that is required is a simple inventory of their friends and "friends of friends." If we really stretch this network, there usually is someone who might be able to lend a helping hand.

There are also people who aren't really directly connected but may know someone who might be able to help. By openly sharing concerns with others, we create a situation where new connections may emerge—sometimes in the strangest ways. The key point of this discussion is openness and communication. When people express their needs to others, there are opportunities for help to emerge.

The existing "pool" of contacts is only the beginning point of career development. The "pool" can be expanded by initiating new contacts and by conducting information interviews. Earlier, in the discussion of the case study, the suggestion was made to Amanda that she should engage in some informational interviewing.

This process involves a number of questions about the workplace and usually ends with the following question: "Do you know anyone else whom it would be helpful for me to interview?" In this way, the list of contacts continues to grow. It is also easier to make contact with others when there is a direct referral from someone else.

Another way to look at labor market options is to assume greater personal responsibility for creating work opportunities. There are many aspects of the job search process that are essentially passive in nature. Given the changing nature of the workplace, there is often a need to take a more proactive stance. Bissonnette (1994) suggests that job searchers learn proposal-making skills as well as constructing resumes. She describes the process as follows:

1. Identify the needs an applicant can fill, given his or her skills and abilities.
2. Identify businesses that have that need, and either don't know it or haven't acted on it yet. Businesses that have either or both characteristics represent the applicant's potential job market.
3. Propose employment to potential employers by defining the needs and presenting the value and benefit of hiring someone to meet them. (p. 32)

Bissonnette (2000) gives the example of a tailor from Vietnam, an older worker who had difficulty finding employment. He noticed that in his area there were several hospitals. In a hospital, there are many people wearing uniforms, and there is a constant need for sending material out for adjustments. While there is considerable work to be done, usually there is not enough work to establish a regular full-time job. The client approached several hospitals with a proposal and ended up piecing together enough work for full-time involvement. By being proactive and approaching the hospitals with a proposal, the tailor was able to meet his needs.

Being proactive in the labor market also means exploring the possibility of becoming an entrepreneur. Some of the personal qualities associated with entrepreneurial actions are as follows: adventurous, confident, persistent, organized, flexible, independent, energetic, positive, hard-working, risk-taking, open-minded, friendly, and achiever (Bird, 1989). The entrepreneurial option is one that fits many people. It also is a direction that people can pursue in geographical areas where there are few traditional job opportunities.

SUMMARY

In this chapter, we have focused on contextual issues and the personal labor market. These factors are a continuation of the process of exploration begun in Chapter 6. To conduct a broadly based exploration, one must look at both the self and the external world, and integrate information from both perspectives.

As exploration proceeds it is not uncommon to have new problems emerge. Adjustments may need to be made. The career counseling process is not linear, and it is quite common to make changes along the way.

In the next chapter we will examine how websites can be used to further the career counseling process. We live in a cyber world, and career counseling is increasingly becoming a part of this new reality. There are exciting new career exploration tools to explore and ways to integrate web-based learning with more traditional career counseling processes. As with any new development, there also are cautions and ethical issues to be discussed. In Chapter 10 we will return to the counseling process with a focus on the formulation of a plan of action.

CHAPTER 8

Using Websites in Support of Career Counseling

- **Deciding Whether to Use a Technology-Based Intervention**

- **Selecting Systems and Sites**

The computer entered the field of career counseling as an important technological tool in the late 1960s. At that time, several developers—Donald E. Super, David V. Tiedeman, Martin Katz, JoAnn Harris-Bowlsbey, and others—created career guidance systems that were designed to replicate what a well-trained career counselor would do and say to help a client with the normal developmental process of choosing an occupation, learning about it in detail, and choosing an educational path related to it (Super, 1970). These systems offered a systematic sequence of activities, including online assessment, database searches, extensive occupational and educational databases, and individual user records that stored demographic data about students and the results of their use of the system. These records allowed students to recall data from their previous uses and provided reports for counselors so that they could follow through with students following their use of the system. Though the earliest systems were developed for students in high school, effort then turned to developing systems to meet the unique developmental needs of students in middle school, students in college, and eventually the general adult public. In the 1970s, a federal agency called the National Occupational Information Coordinating Committee (NOICC) began to fund and promote the development of state career information delivery systems. Similar in many ways to the career guidance systems previously mentioned, these systems featured state-specific labor market information, including salaries and employment outlook. They typically did not store user information and did not offer an integrated career guidance treatment. Their focus was on the quality, extensiveness, and localization of occupational and educational information, and most did not include the online assessment content provided by the early career guidance systems.

Both of these kinds of systems existed as computer software that was installed on a local stand-alone machine or a group of networked computers, first on giant mainframe computers, then on minicomputers, and finally—in the 1980s—on microcomputers. The availability of the Internet as a delivery medium in the 1990s gave rise to the third and current generation of computer-based services that we know today—systems and sites available on the Internet.

The total array of resources available on the Internet can be viewed in three groups:

- **Comprehensive systems** that include the storage of a user record, online assessment, searches, databases, and strategies to synthesize data in ways useful for decision making. Such systems—exemplified by the *Kuder Career Planning System* and DISCOVER—have the characteristics and content previously described for career guidance systems. The term *user record* has been replaced by the term *portfolio* and, in the case of the *Kuder Career Planning System* at least, this portfolio is a lifelong one, stored on a secure server by a unique user ID and password and accessible by the user from any place where access to the Internet is possible. Today's technology allows the addition of audio, video, animation, exciting graphics, and avatars (a guide used to explain the functionality of a given screen or to explain something, such as a score report.) The existence of these features makes it feasible to develop interesting content for elementary-age students.

- **Partial systems** that include some combination of the storage of a user record (a career portfolio), online assessment, and databases but do not include all of the components needed for sequential career guidance. Examples of such systems are sites that include, for example, online assessment plus the provision of a list of occupations and their descriptions, such as Career Key (www.careerkey.org). Another example would be a site that provides a search of postsecondary schools and their descriptions, such as Peterson's Publishing (www.petersons.com). Other examples are the sites that allow the posting of a resume and a search for jobs, such as MonsterBoard (www.monster.com) or the Department of Labor site that provides career information for students in Grades K-12 (http://www.bls.gov/k12/index.htm).
- **Websites** that provide one important component of the career planning process—such as a database of occupational descriptions (exemplified by the O*Net occupational database at http://online.onetcenter.org/) or a list of postsecondary schools such as the National Center for Educational Statistics postsecondary school site at http://nces.ed.gov/ipeds)—but are not linked in any way to a total career planning process for a given user.

Research over the years (Taber & Luzzo, 1999) has consistently provided evidence that the most effective assistance for clients is a combination of support from counselors and from technology. Not even the most comprehensive system will be maximally effective if used without the support of a knowledgeable career counselor. Logic, combined with research evidence, suggests that the less integrated and comprehensive a system is, the more involved the career counselor needs to be.

Given the current advanced state of Internet-delivered systems and sites, this chapter will provide some guidelines about how career counselors can determine whether to use technology-based interventions, how to select them, and how to support their use with clients and students.

DECIDING WHETHER TO USE A TECHNOLOGY-BASED INTERVENTION

There are at least two criteria that are effective in determining whether to use a technology-based intervention: the presenting problem of the client and the readiness of the client. In Chapter 5, we discussed the process of working with a client to identify the needs and specific goals that are to be addressed in the counseling relationship. Once these are determined, the career counselor can make a judgment about whether a technology-based intervention is appropriate. Web-based systems and sites may provide effective service in three areas: (1) online assessment of interests, skills, work values, and personality type as these relate to career choices; (2) searches through extensive databases to identify possible alternatives; and (3) information about myriad options and topics that pertain to career choice and planning. Further, the existence of a long-term career portfolio offers a unique opportunity to synthesize many aspects of the career exploration and planning process as well as to share parts of it with potential employers or school admission officers. Let us consider these capabilities one at a time.

If a client's needs include assessment of self-characteristics that relate to career choice, there are at least two kinds of interventions: informal assessment and formal assessment. Informal assessment, described in Chapter 5, may be in the form of a structured interview, checklists, card sorts, guided imagery, or guided activities. Formal assessment—instruments that have been developed with scientific rigor—may be administered in print-, computer-, or web-based form. Computer- or web-based administration has the advantages of not requiring counselor time for administration, eliminating scoring errors or omissions of responses, and providing immediate feedback to the client. Computer-based administration may have the disadvantage of leading the client to put too much faith in the results of the assessment because of an unwarranted perception that the computer has some magic power.

A very wide array of inventories of interest, skills, abilities, values, and personality type exist. There is a fee associated with online use of almost all of the assessment instruments that have been developed with scientific rigor. Exceptions are those that have been developed with public funding such as the O*Net Interest Profiler, O*Net Work Importance Locator, and ASVAB Interest Finder. The executable computer code for the O*Net instruments can be downloaded without charge from their site, http://online.onetcenter.org. The results of no-fee Armed Services Vocational Aptitude Battery (ASVAB) instruments taken in print form can be entered in order to identify occupations at http://www.asvabprogram.com.

If a client needs to search large databases in order to identify items that have desired characteristics—such as databases of vocational–technical schools, colleges, or jobs—a technology-based intervention is the preferred method of intervention, far surpassing the ability of print-based materials or the career counselor to meet this information need. The O*Net occupational database, available at http://online.onetcenter.org, contains very complete descriptions of all occupations in the United States and is constantly updated and maintained by the U.S. Department of Labor. This database is searchable by industry, keyword, and on a related Department of Labor site, CareerInfoNet (www.acinet.org), by level of education, demand, and income. Similarly, the complete list of postsecondary schools approved by the National Center for Educational Statistics is available at http://nces.ed.gov/collegenavigator/ and allows a search of the entire database by multiple characteristics.

If a client needs information about topics related to educational and career planning, carefully selected websites are likely to be the preferred sources. The options and topics may include information about financial aid sources, employers, resume writing, job interviewing, and many others. Of course, information on these topics is also available in print materials, but the Internet offers the potential for constant update and for use of videos and multiple linkages to other sources of information. The first step when deciding whether to use a technology-based intervention is to identify the needs of the client. Examples of common topics that a career counselor might deal with, that are not best served by a technology-based intervention, include the following:

- learning how to manage one's career
- learning how to get along with coworkers or a supervisor
- deciding how to balance the demands of work and other life roles
- knowing how to prioritize and make decisions about alternatives, once they are identified
- clarifying and strengthening the self-concept

These, and many other needs and concerns, are best addressed through counselor-delivered intervention strategies rather than technology-delivered means.

Suppose that some or all of a client's concerns relate to assessment, database searching, and information-gathering. What else does a counselor need to consider? Krumboltz (1991) and Sampson, Peterson, Lenz, Reardon, & Saunders (1996) remind us that clients may neither be able nor be ready to use self-information and other kinds of information because they hold irrational beliefs that serve as a barrier to effective use. Krumboltz identified irrational beliefs related to a client's current career situation, what seems necessary for happiness, factors that should influence decisions, changes that can be made, and efforts that can be initiated. Sampson et al. describe irrational thoughts such as thinking that absolute certainty is a necessity before taking any action related to career or that a career decision must last for a lifetime. In an introductory interview, such as that described in Chapter 5, a counselor may be able to identify such barriers or may choose to administer a short inventory such as the *Career Beliefs Inventory* (Krumboltz, 1991) or the *Career Thoughts Inventory* (Sampson et al., 1996). Use of assessment, database searching, and information-gathering in any medium will be enhanced when irrational beliefs have been removed as a barrier.

A second important client characteristic to consider is learning style. Some individuals learn well from technology-based interventions, learning through reading, perhaps enhanced by pictures, audio, and video. Other people prefer to learn through social contact, and those clients may profit from additional methods of interventions such as group counseling, a classroom approach, one-on-one counseling, job-shadowing, and informational interviewing.

Several professional organizations—the National Career Development Association (NCDA), the American Counseling Association (ACA), and the National Board for Certified Counselors (NBCC)—have developed ethical guidelines for the use of web-based interventions. One of those guidelines, though it is difficult to follow, is that the counselor should be confident that a client can profit from a technology-based intervention before assigning him or her to it. Meeting this guideline appears to be a combination of (1) an appropriate fit between a client concern and the content of a specific system or site, (2) a client's readiness to receive and make effective use of information, and (3) a client's ability to learn in computer-delivered ways and to be comfortable in doing so. If a counselor's decision to use technology as an intervention is guided by these three principles, the ethical standard is met, assuming that the systems and sites used meet other ethical standards. If the client does not profit from use of technology after application of these standards, another guideline applies; one which requires a counselor to make a change in strategy, dealing with the problem through face-to-face career counseling or some other method of human intervention.

SELECTING SYSTEMS AND SITES

Given the thousands of websites that offer some kind of career assistance or information, how can a counselor know which sites to use? The best answer to this question is to follow this sequence of steps:

1. From your experience with your typical clients, and with their feedback, make a list of their needs and information concerns. This list might include the following:
   - What are my interests?
   - What are my skills?
   - How can I transfer the skills I have to another job?
   - How can I write a good resume?
   - How can I find a job?
   - How can I learn about an employer?
   - How can I find a school?
   - How can I get financial aid?
   - How can I network with others?
   - How can I learn about the GRE (or other tests)?
   - How can I learn the details of an occupation?

2. Use reference books written by respected professionals in the career development field to identify one or more websites or systems that address each of the questions on your list. Such reference books include the following:
   - Harris-Bowlsbey, J., Riley Dikel, M., & Sampson, J. P. Jr. (2002). *The Internet: A Tool for Career Planning*, 2nd ed. Tulsa, OK: National Career Development Association.
   - Riley Dikel, M., & Roehm, F. (2006). *The Guide to Internet Job Searching: 2006–2007*. Chicago, IL: VGM Career Horizons.

   Also, consult the website of the National Career Development Association at www.ncda.org, which maintains an updated list of sites that have been reviewed for quality. If you have topics on your list not covered in reference books, search for these topics by using a search engine such as that provided at www.metacrawler.com. Enter two or three search words relating to the topic, and a list of applicable sites will be provided.

3. Take the time to use the systems and sites you have identified, asking questions such as the following:
   - Was the site developed by persons or organizations that are respected by the career development profession as qualified sources for this type of assessment or information? Are the developers identified?

- If it is an assessment site, was the assessment instrument developed by a known professional in the field? Is information provided about reliability, validity, and utility with diverse populations in computer-delivered mode?
- Is the site updated and maintained? If it provides data, does the site indicate when it was last updated? Are there changes and enhancements to the site from time to time?
- Is the site user-friendly? Is it easy to navigate? Is its appearance attractive? Is its reading level appropriate for the population you have? Does the site make effective use of color, graphics, videos, or other visual enhancements?
- If a user record of some kind is kept, what data about the user is collected, for how long, and with what kind of security? The answer to this question is difficult to get and may require an email to customer service or a phone call.
- Is there a cost for the assessment or service provided? If so, what is the cost? Can a lower cost be negotiated for volume use through an arrangement with its publisher?

4. Select a finite list of sites for your use and get to know them well. Sites change often, and for that reason it is necessary to review them periodically.
5. Print out the home page or a menu from each site, and make multiple copies for use with clients. When you ask a client to use a system or site, be very specific about the assignment. It may be helpful to highlight, on the printout, the specific option(s) that should be taken by the client.
6. Follow through with the client after use of the system or site. If the assignment was some kind of online career assessment, obtain a copy of the results and discuss their meanings with the client. If the assignment was a database search, discuss the search variables used to produce the list of occupations, schools, or financial aid sources provided by the search. Discuss the reasons for selecting these particular search variables and the client's responses to the resulting list of options. Assist the client to form criteria for reducing the list and prioritizing the remaining options. If the assignment was to collect information about occupations, schools, or other topics, review the information with the client and assist with understanding the meaning of the information as it applies to personal career choices.

AN EXAMPLE

Chris came to his counselor at his high school during his junior year asking for help with learning about occupations and making some possible choices. After an initial interview; during which the counselor learned about the student's family, career influences, school record, and work experience; the counselor provided a brief explanation, supported by a one-page handout, of the six Holland types and of the fact that occupations can be categorized into the same six types. Then he asked the client to use the University of Missouri website (http://career.missouri.edu/students/explore/thecareerinterestsgame.php) before the next interview and gave him a short instruction sheet that contained the URL and directions to read the descriptions of the six types, to select the two that appealed to him most, and to view and print the list of occupations and their descriptions. The counselor asked Chris to bring the printout with him to the next interview and indicated that they would look at it together.

At the beginning of the second interview, the counselor asked Chris to take a few minutes to do the *O*Net Work Importance Profiler*, a values card sort that he had downloaded and printed from the O*Net site (www.onetcenter.org/WIP.html). Chris did this card sort in about eight minutes and identified Achievement and Independence as his two highest work values. When Chris and the counselor studied the titles and descriptions of six occupations that Chris had chosen from the lists associated with Holland's Investigative environment (Chris' first choice) and Realistic environment (Chris' second choice), it became clear that two of the occupations offered a much greater potential for achievement and independence than the others. The counselor asked Chris to research these two occupations thoroughly in preparation for the next session and gave him directions for use of two websites—the *Occupational Outlook Handbook* (www.bls.gov/oco) and *CareerInfoNet* (www.acinet.org), maintained by the U.S. Department of Labor. Both provide accurate and updated information about occupations. Further, he helped Chris find two people from the local Lions' Club who work in each of these occupations and encouraged him to make an appointment for an informational interview with each of them. He also gave Chris a list of sample questions to ask during the informational interview and asked him to return in two weeks with all of this accumulated information.

At the third interview two weeks later, Chris and the counselor reviewed all of the information collected about these two occupations. The counselor assisted Chris to examine how each related to his interests, the academic requirements for entry, and the potential for each to satisfy the identified values. This work resulted in placing these two occupations in priority order. Chris and the counselor then began to identify postsecondary majors related to these two occupations and schools in the state that offered both of these majors, leaving time for choosing one occupation over the other later. In preparation for the next interview, the counselor asked Chris to access the website of the identified colleges, specifically the section that describes their majors, including required courses, descriptions of those courses, and follow-up data about the employment of students who have graduated in each major field within the past five years. Further, the counselor asked Chris to make an appointment with the department chair of each of the two major fields at the university and gave him a list of questions to ask.

At the fourth interview, Chris returned with a great deal of information about the two majors. Further, he stated that he was ready to plan to attend the state university, declare a major in one of the two fields, and fill in electives with selected courses from the other. He also stated that he felt very certain about his decisions.

SUMMARY

The use of web-based career guidance systems and stand-alone websites can be very beneficial to career planning for clients who are ready to deal with information, able to learn through the medium of technology, and have needs for assessment, database searching, and/or information-gathering. In order to achieve maximum effectiveness, however, a counselor needs to be very knowledgeable about the systems and sites being suggested to students and to stay involved in the student's process. Assignments given to the student need to be specific and on target with his or her needs. Further, the important component of ongoing counselor support needs to be maintained for the purpose of assisting the client to turn data into personally meaningful information that guides decision making.

CHAPTER 9

Building and Using a Virtual Career Center

- **Components of a Virtual Career Center**
- **Local Information as a Part of the Virtual Career Center**
- **Access to Web Counseling**
- **Monitoring Feature**
- **Organization of the Virtual Career Center**
- **Sample Sites**

The previous chapter discussed the topic of web-based systems and sites, identifying their characteristics and strengths. That chapter also provided some guidelines for determining when a student or client can profit from the use of a website and how counselors can support such use through one-on-one counseling or through a group process. This chapter takes that theme one step further by describing how career interventions can be provided through a portal that provides an integrated system of websites combined with counseling support provided by electronic means.

The virtual career center is a new tool for assisting clients in the 21st century. Like a physical career center, a virtual career center can be defined as a site, or portal, that provides access to sources of information and assistance needed for career planning that are organized as an integrated whole. This system of organization must make sense to the person who accesses the virtual career center. Sampson et al. (2001) proposes that the site's content may be either resource-based or needs-based. A later section of this chapter will discuss these two methods of organization.

First, let's examine some of the advantages and disadvantages of building a comprehensive virtual career center. One obvious advantage is that clients who access it can do so from any system connected to the Internet and at any hour of any day. Another advantage is that such a center does not require physical space: real resources such as books, videos, and computers loaded with software; or on-site staff. A third advantage is that the site may be programmed so that it has the capability to guide the users through the resources and assist them with their analysis. A fourth advantage is that some clients feel more comfortable accessing a technology-based resource than talking to career counselors or others who may staff physical career centers.

Of course, there are also disadvantages of virtual career centers. Some clients prefer and profit more from personal attention and interaction. A physical career center may offer the opportunity to ask questions of a knowledgeable person face to face and to profit from the facilitative skills that the person may apply. Further, a physical center provides the potential and facilities to invite real guests in, including potential employers and representatives of schools that the students may be considering for the future. Such a center also provides the physical space and opportunity to offer instruction and small group work on topics such as resume writing and job interviewing.

COMPONENTS OF A VIRTUAL CAREER CENTER

There are four components of a fully featured virtual career center: links to existing websites, locally developed information, access to web counseling, and an overall monitoring function. We'll begin with links to screened and appropriate websites that already exist. The career planning process entails at least four broad topics: assessment of self-variables related to career choices, occupational search and information, educational search and information, and job search and information. Thus, one part of the virtual career center would consist of brief descriptions and links to one or more sites in each of these categories that the designer of the center has thoroughly screened. An increasing number of states (including Nebraska, Missouri, South Carolina, Kansas, Tennessee, and Arkansas) currently offer comprehensive career guidance websites without fee to the schools, agencies, and individual citizens of their states; typically the cost of developing and maintaining these sites is paid by the state department of education, perhaps in conjunction with the state department of labor, workforce development division. In such states, schools and agencies already have a rich core of web-based services available that offer substantive assistance in all four of these areas. Indeed, these sites can be incorporated into virtual career centers, though the online assessment component of the systems will not be free of charge to people who do not live in these states.

In order to offer the assessment component, links can be made to no-fee sites—such as the *University of Missouri's Career Interests* game (http://career.missouri.edu/students/explore/thecareerinterestsgame.php) or to for-fee sites—such as the *Kuder Career Planning System* (www.kuder.com) site with its interests, skills, and work values inventories or the *Self-Directed Search* site (www.self-directed-search.com), offering this interest inventory and its full interpretation. As detailed in *The Internet: A Tool for Career Counseling* (Harris-Bowlsbey, et al., 2002) and on its ongoing online update at www.ncda.org, there are many sites that provide assessment. A counselor incorporating these sites into a virtual center has the ethical responsibility to know the guidelines for the use of web-based assessment and to request information from publishers related to those guidelines. Publishers of for-fee sites will typically negotiate a volume fee for use of their site that is considerably lower than the per-person fee posted on the site.

Assessment sites typically provide a list of occupations for consideration as a result of taking an online inventory. Also, they typically link the user from occupations provided in the list to the descriptions provided in the online *Occupational Outlook Handbook* (www.bls.gov/oco) or some other definitive source of occupational information. The *Occupational Outlook Handbook*, a publication of the U.S. Department of Labor, offers comprehensive descriptions of approximately 250 occupations. A second, very valuable Department of Labor site is CareerInfoNet (www.acinet.org). This site offers several sections of information about hundreds of occupations, including employment outlook; state and national salary levels; required knowledge, skills, and abilities; tasks and activities; links to education and training opportunities; and other online resources for job-related information. Unique features are the availability of short videos about each occupation, state-level salary and job-demand information, and the capability to enter scores from a variety of assessment inventories in order to develop a list of occupations for exploration. The most comprehensive of all web-based sources for occupational information is the U.S. Department of Labor's O*Net database, accessible at http://online.onetcenter.org.

Many students and adults are seeking information about schools where they can get further education or training in one specific specialty. For this reason, a virtual career center would include links to sites that offer a comprehensive search of schools, such as the National Center for Educational Statistics' IPEDS site (http://nces.ed.gov/ipeds/org), the RWM Vocational School Database (www.rwm.org/rwm), or the Peterson's site (www.petersons.com) that includes a graduate school database. Because many students need financial aid, this section of the virtual center should include a link to the official U.S. Department of Education site (http://studentaid.ed.gov/PORTALSWebApp/students/english/index.jsp), which describes all federal student assistance programs and their application procedures. The site also includes the online Free Application for Federal Student Aid (FAFSA), a requirement for applying for student financial aid, in both English and Spanish.

There are hundreds of sites that assist clients to learn job-seeking skills and search large databases of job openings. They are of varying quality; some require a fee for posting a resume and using the database and some do not. One site that provides a broad range of information about the job-seeking process is that maintained by Richard Bolles, author of *What Color Is Your Parachute?* at www.jobhuntersbible.com. Bolles' site includes such topics as how to use the Internet for job hunting, how to use the results of assessment, linkages to relevant online articles, resume writing, databases of job listings, and a host of other topics. Another site that provides a great deal of general job search information, especially for new college graduates, is that maintained by the National Association of Colleges and Employers at www.jobweb.com. At this site, topics such as resume writing, job interviews, intern employers, and links to hundreds of articles of interest to college graduates are included. Still another immensely useful site for job seekers is that maintained by Margaret Riley-Dikel called the Riley Guide at (http://www.rileyguide.com). This site is continuously updated and is a comprehensive resource to Internet job bank sites and information about job searching, resume writing, interviewing, salary negotiation, and many other topics related to the job search. Some of the most prominent sites for job searching are Monster.com (www.monster.com), CareerBuilder (www.careerbuilder.com), and College Grad Job Hunter (www.collegegrad.com). Most states have a job bank supported by their state department of labor where employers list jobs daily and where job seekers can post their resumes. Some sites, such as Indeed (http://www.indeed.com), offer the capability of a powerful "spider," a computer program that searches multiple sites and pulls the resultant findings into one list.

The sites mentioned above are examples of desirable sites to make available to users of a virtual career center. There are hundreds of other possibilities, many of which are listed on NCDA's website at www.ncda.org in the section titled "Resources," under the menu item "Internet Sites for Career Planning." Other sites that contain a comprehensive list of career-related sites are the U.S. Department of Employment Security's *CareerInfoNet* (www.acinet.org) and the Bolles site (www.jobhuntersbible.com), both described above. Counselors designing virtual career centers should become knowledgeable about these sites; review them against current ethical guidelines (see www.nbcc.org. and www.ncda.org, sites that provide guidelines); and select a few that have high-quality content for their target populations. Because staying updated on the content and navigation of these sites is a time-consuming and necessary task, selecting a few and doing a good job with them is preferable to attempting to be all-encompassing.

LOCAL INFORMATION AS A PART OF THE VIRTUAL CAREER CENTER

Websites offer the powerful capability to post information local to the developer and pertinent only to the specific target population addressed. For a virtual career center, the following are examples of such local information:

- Information about the career placement or counseling center, including its services, location, staff, and hours of operation.
- Information about workshops (such as those on resume writing or job interviewing) or other services that could be helpful with career planning.
- Description of the institution's majors, which are organized by the same classification system used in the interest inventory taken by clients and for classification of occupations. For example, if the online interest inventories give the user a Holland code, then the institution's majors should be accessible under the local information part of the site, organized by Holland codes, and should include descriptions. These descriptions might also be linked to the e-mail addresses of academic advisors or faculty who could provide additional information to the student.
- Information about employers who hire the institution's graduates or who may be coming to campus to interview prospective employees.
- Information about alumni who are willing to serve as e-mail mentors and the capability to link up with them electronically.

ACCESS TO WEB COUNSELING

The ethical standards proposed by the National Board for Certified Counselors (NBCC) define web counseling as "the practice of professional counseling and information delivery that occurs when client(s) and counselor are in separate or remote locations and utilize electronic means to communicate over the Internet" (NBCC, 2007). In today's technology, there are three ways in which such communication may take place: asynchronous e-mail, synchronous e-mail, and videoconferencing. In asynchronous e-mail communication, the counselor and client exchange e-mail messages that are read and responded to at different times. In synchronous e-mail communication, the counselor and the client are at their respective computers at the same time and communicate in real time. In videoconferencing, the machines of both the counselor and the client are equipped with hardware and software that allows them to see each other and hear each other during the exchange. Obviously, the client–counselor interaction could take place by telephone rather than through computers.

Statements of ethical standards propose stringent guidelines for web counseling. The following are some examples from three different sets of guidelines, indicating counselor responsibilities:

- Develop an appropriate intake procedure for potential clients to determine whether online counseling is appropriate for the needs of the client (ACA, 1999).
- Provide clients with a schedule of times during which online counseling services will be available, including reasonable anticipated response times, and provide clients with an alternate means of contacting the professional at other times, including in the event of emergencies (ACA, 1999).
- Define several items (credentials, goals of counseling, agreed-upon cost for services, how unethical behavior can be reported, etc.) in writing to the client in a document that can be downloaded from the Internet or faxed to the client (NCDA, 1997).
- Develop individual online counseling plans that are consistent with both the client's individual circumstances and the limitations of online counseling (ACA, 1999).
- The Internet counselor informs Internet clients of encryption methods being used to help insure the security of client/counselor/supervisor communications (NBCC, 2007).
- Inform clients if, how, and how long session data are being preserved (NBCC, 2007).
- In situations where it is difficult to verify the identity of the Internet client, steps are taken to address impostor concerns, such as by using code words or numbers (NBCC, 2007).
- Within the limits of readily available technology, Internet counselors have an obligation to make their website a barrier-free environment to clients with disabilities (NBCC, 2007).
- Provide links to websites of all appropriate certification bodies and licensure boards to facilitate consumer protection (NBCC, 2007).
- Assure that the client who is requesting service can profit from it in this mode (NCDA, 1997).
- Periodically monitor the client's progress via telephone or videophone teleconference (NCDA, 1997).
- As a part of the counseling orientation process, the Internet counselor collaborates with the Internet client to identify an appropriately trained professional who can provide local assistance, including crisis intervention, if needed. The Internet counselor and Internet client should also collaborate to determine the local crisis hotline telephone number and the local emergency telephone number (NBCC, 2007)
- Refer clients to one or more qualified counselors in their geographic area for face-to-face service if progress is not occurring in electronic mode (NCDA, 1997).

Complete versions of these three ethical statements can be found at the websites of the three professional organizations that developed them: the American Counseling Association (ACA) (www.counseling.org), the National Career Development

Association (NCDA) (www.ncda.org), and the National Board for Certified Counselors (NBCC) (www.nbcc.org).

The NBCC offers training to certified counselors who wish to specialize in web-based counseling, called Distance Counseling. A list of those who have completed this training and are deemed qualified to provide counseling service in this mode is posted on the NBCC website. Administrators in sites who desire to provide a virtual career counseling center should assure that their counselors have this specialized training. Further, there are websites that broker the services of such counselors (such as www.readyminds.com), and counseling services could be integrated by means of a linkage or arrangement with these sites.

MONITORING FEATURE

Ideally, a virtual career center would also have a monitoring feature that builds an integrated record for each user and summarizes that record for both the site user and the counselor, with appropriate user sign-off. Such a feature would have to be designed and programmed at the local level for a given site. The monitoring feature might serve the following functions, storing data into a record for each user:

- Administering a short intake questionnaire, designed to identify the user's needs in order to suggest relevant parts of the website for use.
- Capturing data from external websites used by the client so that information—such as results of assessment, titles of occupations researched, names of schools identified through a search, or a summary of other information gleaned through the research—can be stored within the user's local record.
- Capturing data from the use of locally developed information available on the site, such as titles of majors researched.
- Building a user's summary—such as decisions made, additional research to engage in, or future questions to ask—of interactions with a web counselor. The client should be able to print the summary, and the counselor should also be able to print it—with the client's permission.

ORGANIZATION OF THE VIRTUAL CAREER CENTER

As previously indicated, Sampson et al. (2001) describes two methods of organization for virtual career centers: resource-based and needs-based. A resource-based center is organized by topic. For example, a menu may list topics such as the following:

- Self-assessment
- Majors offered by the university
- Graduate school search and information

- Job-seeking skills
- Effective resumes
- Effective job interviews
- Salary negotiations

A needs-based approach typically has three levels: a menu of possible users (such as middle school student, high school student, college student, adult career changer); a menu of typical needs of each subpopulation, likely developed through focus groups with these populations (such as deciding about occupations, choosing a major, entering an internship, getting the first real job, etc., for college students); and links to resource materials that may provide assistance with a given need.

It would also be possible to organize the content of a virtual career center around the career planning process. Harris-Bowlsbey et al. (2002) proposes a seven-step, cyclical process as follows:

1. Become aware of the need to make choices.
2. Take a snapshot of yourself.
3. Identify occupational alternatives.
4. Get information about identified alternatives.
5. Choose among alternatives.
6. Get the required education or training.
7. Get a job.

Most, if not all, internal or external information could be linked to one or more of these seven steps; and their accomplishment could be supported by web counseling as needed.

SAMPLE SITES

There is an increasing number of virtual career centers, especially at the college–university level. Let's review a couple of those as examples. The first is an outstanding example of a no-fee, university-based virtual career center: the Florida State University site at www.career.fsu.edu. This is a needs-based site with a sidebar menu containing the following options:

- Current/future students
- Alumni
- Employers
- Community members
- Family members
- Faculty/staff
- Career services professionals

Detailing all of the submenus associated with this main menu would consume too much space, so two illustrations are provided: the submenu for those who indicate that they are current students and the submenu for alumni. These menus are as follows:

For current/future students
- Choose a major
- Explore careers
- Consider further education
- Get experience
- Document my skills and experience
- Find a job
- Find FSU undergraduate and graduate student resources

For alumni
- Explore careers
- Consider further education
- Document my skills and experience
- Find a job
- Partner with the Career Center

In turn, each of these menu options leads to additional submenus and then to either locally developed information or external, screened websites. The site offers a phenomenal amount of information for career planning, organized in a way that reduces the information overload for the user. Though the site provides information about how to get face-to-face service at the FSU career center, it does not currently offer the opportunity for online web counseling.

ReadyMinds (www.readyminds.com), a commercial site, is a good illustration of a site that offers access to web counseling. The site offers a customized career counseling service that includes telecounseling (by telephone) and online communication. Professional career counselors broker their services through this site to college students and adults who present a variety of career-related concerns. Web clients may choose available counselors from the database, which provides diversity by specialty, racial–ethnic background, gender, and age. The counselor and the client agree on goals for the counseling. This site either could be used as a stand-alone site or could be included in a virtual career center design in order to add this component to one developed by a university or an organization.

SUMMARY

This chapter has discussed four potential components of an integrated virtual career center: links to existing, screened websites; locally developed information; access to web counseling; and an overall site monitoring function. Further, each of these components has been discussed in some detail, ethical standards have been reviewed, and two sample sites have been described.

CHAPTER

Consolidation, Decision Making, and Action Planning

- **Consolidation**
- **Decision Making**
- **Readiness for Action Planning**
- **Developing the Action Plan**
- **Advocacy and Social Action**

Through relationship building and exploration, a considerable amount of information is generated. While this is a necessary part of the process, there comes a time when the information needs to be pulled together and focused toward action. This consolidation develops in different ways and is an integral part of the career counseling process.

Some career counselors try to force consolidation too early and end up with plans that have little chance of success because clients have not been part of the process. There are many reasons for this push towards counselor-generated plans. Sometimes it is just a matter of experience and of seeing connections that clients do not seem to understand. In this scenario, it may seem more expedient to show the patterns and to introduce action plans. In other situations there is pressure to "get the job done" and to move on to other tasks. This "hurry up" work ethic leads career counselors to press for understanding and action and to sometimes get far ahead of their clients. Whether the source of this pressure is internally or externally generated, there is little doubt that the end result can be compromised by moving too quickly.

It is important that clients feel a real sense of ownership as they attempt to better understand themselves (identify patterns), to make decisions, and to generate action plans. Without this form of involvement there is little chance that significant change will be realized. While there may be some form of verbal agreement, this usually doesn't translate into sufficient motivation to generate ongoing change.

In this chapter we will be addressing the issues of consolidation, decision making, and action planning. As information is consolidated, there is an opportunity for more self-understanding, which lays the foundation for decision making and action planning.

CONSOLIDATION

Considerable information is generated in the exploration phase. There are certain patterns that need to be identified, and perhaps clarified, within this information. This consolidation process requires close collaboration between client and counselor. The communication process that seems to work best is one in which there is a gradual move from nondirective to more directive counselor statements. The ideal situation is one in which the client identifies patterns and pulls the information together by herself. There will be times when more direction is needed. This requires a second step. At this level, the career counselor draws attention to some important pieces of information but avoids any specific conclusions. Even with this form of leading question, the connections will not always be made. If there is a need to move further, the counselor is more direct but still frames the question in a tentative manner. The following example illustrates the process:

Background: Judith is working in the banking industry. She is frustrated with her inability to make progress within the organization and discusses her situation with a career counselor. She works hard and has good relationships with some colleagues. Nevertheless, she always seems to be passed over for important transfers or promotions. As the counselor delves further into her experiences, it becomes apparent that she has some difficulty relating to supervisors, managers, or anyone in a position of authority. With this background in mind, consider how the following client–counselor dialogue develops.

Counselor	It seems that you are really frustrated by some of your experiences in the firm.
Judith	Yes, I am starting to feel that I just need to get out and look for something else.
Counselor	As you look at what is happening, can you see any patterns?
Judith	Well, it seems that I just keep running into incompetent managers.
Counselor	You do seem to have more difficulty working with the managers. When you describe your relationships with other colleagues you seem more positive.
Judith	I have lots of friends in the company. It's just the managers that cause me grief.
Counselor	I wonder if there is anything different about the way in which relationships develop with the managers?
Judith	Hmmm. That's an interesting question. Maybe I do act differently. I try to be the same with everyone but I know that sometimes I freeze when I talk with them.
Counselor	What do you think is happening for you in your meetings with the managers?
Judith	I don't know, I just become so self-conscious. I feel like I'm always being judged, like my work isn't good enough.
Counselor	And what happens then?
Judith	I just go into a shell, I don't say anything and afterward I get so mad at myself for not speaking up.
Counselor	Is this something that you would like to change?
Judith	Yeah, I guess I have to do something about it. The problem isn't going to go away if I don't deal with it. If I am going to get ahead I need to learn how to work better with managers.

This scenario might have developed very differently if the career counselor had started with a hypothesis and then looked for confirmation. It is possible to be too quick with observations. As was stated earlier, the likelihood of clients following through is much higher if they come up with their own conclusions.

Judith's last sentence contains an important movement forward. Not only is she aware of the problem, but she also wants to do something about it. Patsula (1992) uses the term "contingency" statement to describe this form of readiness. A contingency statement has the following form: "If I am going to address this problem, I need to do the following." While clients may not use these exact words, there is a need to bring them to a place where they not only recognize problems but also see that they need to take some action. Without this realization, there is little chance of moving forward to action planning.

Another aspect of this case scenario is the emergence of metaphors when describing the problem situation. Judith indicates that she "freezes" when she talks with managers. That simple image captures the nature of her relationship with those in authority. It might be helpful to have her create a drawing of what this freezing looks like when she interacts with managers. From there, it is on to discussing ways of "unfreezing." It seems that it is something that she is doing to herself. Her self-talk focuses on being judged and being evaluated negatively. Perhaps with some different cognitive messages, she would view the situation in a different way. The metaphor helps to create a picture that draws together a great deal of information and is also something that can be changed to create a more positive outcome.

DECISION MAKING

As information is pulled together, there are occasions when the move toward action requires certain decisions to be made. Making these decisions usually requires some combination of intuitive and rational processes. For some people, it is simply a matter of "letting it sit for a while." With the passage of time there are opportunities to develop new perspectives and to listen to the more intuitive parts of our being. This can be further enhanced by changing some aspects of the environment (going for a walk or doing something completely different). If we come back to the problem refreshed, we are in a better position to use our creativity and problem-solving capacities.

One of the most common methods of making decisions is simply to make a list of the advantages and disadvantages. Sorting information into categories helps to clarify some situations. It is not always a matter of which list is the longest, because one factor might outweigh all the others in terms of importance. For example, a great job might come up in another city, but if a person really doesn't want to move, this point can be the determining factor.

The Career Wheel that was described in Figure 4.1 can also be used for decision making. In the earlier discussion, the focus was on generating information to fit into each segment of the wheel. Once the wheel is completed, there is the opportunity to view all the information from a more holistic perspective. Upon this foundation it is possible to brainstorm some career options (placed in the center of the wheel). Another way to use the wheel is to start with one option, place it in the center, and see how it fits with other segments of the wheel. For example, one of our clients (Burt) was thinking of returning to school to go into a horticulture program. He had been working for two years after completing high school and was employed in a yard maintenance firm. While the money was satisfactory, he was not entirely satisfied with the job and wanted to look at other options. With the option "returning to school—Horticulture" in the center of the Career Wheel, it was possible to see how this career pathway fit with interests, values, skills, personality, significant others, past educational experiences, work and leisure experiences, and the labor market. For Burt, the option seemed to fit well. The only problem was his high school record. To enroll in the horticulture program he needed to complete a science course at high school level. This then became the first step in his action plan.

Another way to facilitate decision making is to have clients make two lists. On one, they place all the careers that they are considering. On the other, they place the career considerations that are important to them—rank ordered (i.e., wages, location, security, travel opportunities, advancement opportunities, and so on). They then use their list of career considerations (starting with their top ranked items) to eliminate some of the career options that don't fit for them.

The comparison of career options with career considerations can be put into a table and formally used as a grid for reviewing various options. There are various ways of making this grid. The grid in Figure 10.1 from the Career Pathways program (Amundson & Poehnell, 1996) is one possibility.

In this example, the employment counselor option has the highest overall score and is ranked higher than the social work option in the use of abilities, excitement, creativity, and money. The only place where social work has the edge is in terms of helping others. The career options of working in a group home and being a financial worker seem to have far less appeal. The information, laid out in this manner, helps to facilitate further discussion and it can be helpful with regard to decision making.

Decision making is difficult. It can be useful to employ several different approaches. There is a need for both intuitive and rational decision-making.

FIGURE 10.1
Evaluating career options

| (Factors) | (Career Options) | | | |
	1. Social Worker	2. Employment Counselor	3. Counselor in a Group Home	4. Financial Assistance Worker
1. Challenge	+ 5	+ 5	+ 3	+ 2
2. Freedom	+ 4	+ 4	+ 3	+ 1
3. Flexibility	+ 4	+ 4	+ 2	+ 1
4. Use Abilities	+ 2	+ 4	+ 1	0
5. Exciting	+ 2	+ 3	+ 1	0
6. Creativity	+ 2	+ 4	+ 1	0
7. Money	+ 3	+ 4	+ 2	+ 2
8. Reward Hard Work	+ 2	+ 2	+ 1	0
9. Help Others	+ 4	+ 3	+ 2	+ 1
10. Opportunity to Travel	0	0	+ 1	0
Total Score	28	33	17	7

Source: From Career Pathways, *by Norman Amundson and Gray Poehnell, Copyright 1996, Ergon Communications. Used by permission.*

In our fast-paced world, we need to include decision-making strategies that use the full range of our capacity. Gelatt (1989) uses the term "positive uncertainty" to describe a process in which we use balanced, versatile, and whole-brain decision strategies. With this framework there is a move from "either/or" thinking to "both/and" thinking. As we make decisions, we need to be positive about what we are doing, while at the same time maintaining a healthy sense of wariness and uncertainty.

Many people have difficulty making decisions because they want to be absolutely sure about the steps they are taking. With the changing labor market and world events, it is no longer possible to offer this form of assurance (if it ever was). Sometimes the issue isn't what decision to make but is the fact that people have difficulty accepting the uncertainty and unpredictable aspect of our world (Trevor-Roberts, 2006). It is not possible to control all factors. Even in the most ideal situations there is an element of uncertainty. In many instances, people just need to take a step forward, with the understanding that they will need to make changes along the way. Gelatt (1989) uses the term "positive uncertainty" to describe the process of moving forward with a positive attitude while also being prepared for some adaptations in response to changing circumstances. To illustrate this process, consider the problem of those secondary students who have several interests and can't make a decision about what major to have in university. They might be clear about the fact that university is the best option; however, they may be unable to specifically define a long-term career plan. In these circumstances perhaps the best that can be achieved is for them to take a step forward and enroll in university courses, understanding that they may want to change their major after they have more experiences. Career decision-making is not a "one time" event, and in many instances it involves ongoing evaluation and change.

For some students the underlying need for control and certainty might be feelings of fear and vulnerability. If problems are not addressed at the "root" level, there is good possibility that the career counseling process will be undermined.

Another way to view the reality of an "uncertain" world is through the lens of chaos theory (Bloch, 2005; Bright & Pryor, 2005; Pryor & Bright, 2006). This approach emphasizes the chaotic nature of our world, but it also makes the point that even in the most chaotic circumstances there are certain patterns that can emerge. These patterns can come from unexpected sources and often reflect a unique combination of probability (convergent) and possibility (divergent) thinking (Pryor, Amundson, & Bright, in press). There are times when people need to enlarge options, to create new possibilities. And conversely, there are times when some options need to be set aside and the emphasis needs to shift to the more probable outcomes. Effective career counseling relies on the judicious use of both strategies. There are times when people are moving too quickly to career decisions and under these conditions the best decision is often to stop the movement forward and return to a broader exploration of possibilities. There are also other situations where people are stuck in a plethora of possibilities, unable to make a decision. Under these conditions, it might be prudent to focus on the options with the greatest likelihood of success and encourage some movement forward.

READINESS FOR ACTION PLANNING

As people make the move toward action, there are various ways in which the process might be "derailed." We have already discussed instances where counselors got ahead of clients when planning. Rather than mutually determining plans, counselors might move too quickly and find themselves developing plans that lack sufficient client involvement. Under these circumstances, clients often agree to plans but lack the motivation to carry through to the end.

An inability to move toward action planning also occurs in situations where clients insert their needs for certainty and control into the decision-making process. As was just discussed, these actions might be the result of feelings of fear and vulnerability. Rather than continuing the push toward action, it can be more appropriate to delve deeper into the underlying concerns.

Readiness for action planning also can be impacted by the strong positive nature of the counseling relationship. When clients come to career counseling, they find themselves immersed in a relationship where there is acceptance and genuine caring and respect. These facilitating conditions create an environment where exploration and learning can occur. While this positive development can be very encouraging, it also can be difficult to walk away from and can lead to feelings of loss—for counselors as well as for clients. As clients move toward action, they need to feel support and move away from the warmth and the security of the counseling relationship.

The process of disengaging starts at the beginning, when there is the setting of specific goals and a discussion about how many sessions will be needed. If there are multiple sessions, it can be helpful to introduce the idea of closing several weeks before the final session. A statement such as the following can be helpful in making this transition:

> We certainly have been making some good progress. I really like the way in which you have been engaging in this exploration. We have another two sessions. I am hopeful that we will meet our goal.

It also is appropriate to openly discuss feelings of loss and uncertainty as people move forward. Career counselors need to share feelings and treat the ending as a natural part of the process. Some clients begin bargaining at this point and ask for additional sessions. While this may be warranted in some situations, there is often a need to gently bring the process to a close.

DEVELOPING THE ACTION PLAN

When developing action plans, it is important to distinguish between short- and long-term plans. For many clients, the action plan is only one part of a longer journey. Taking the first step can be important to help create the momentum for further action.

When constructing plans, it is important to focus attention on concrete and attainable goals. Gysbers, Heppner, and Johnston (2003) suggest that these goals must fit with the unique situation for each client and also be constructed in such a way that the client perceives them as being reasonable. Walter and Peller (1992) make the following suggestions for developing action plans:

1. Indicate what will be accomplished using positive language.
2. Describe actions using verbs ending in "ing" (writing, calling, researching, and so on).
3. Start with the present and be concrete about what is going to happen after the client leaves the counseling session.
4. Carefully work through all the details, paying particular attention to the time-frame for achieving each task.
5. Focus on those areas that are within the client's control.
6. Use examples and metaphors that fit with the client's experience.

When using these guidelines, it is important that the counselor uses a natural questioning process to help the client specify all the necessary details. For example, suppose that a client decides that the most appropriate action is to send an application to a college. Some details that might need to be addressed are as follows:

1. When will the application form be picked up?
2. When will the application be completed and mailed?
3. When will a second contact be made with the college to ensure that all the material has arrived?

Plans sometimes fail because insufficient attention has been directed toward all the small details.

Another important aspect of action planning is deciding who else needs to be involved. Referrals to other professionals or agencies may need to be made, such as when dealing with challenging people or situations. It is important, when making these referrals, to have some background information about the people and the organizations involved. This personal network is part of your counseling expertise. The best referrals are usually made in situations where the career counselor is well acquainted with the people and services at the other end. The other aspect of this is the fact that counselors need to know their own limitations (personal and educational). See Chapter 1.

It can be helpful to develop a back-up plan as part of the planning process. One would hope that all would go well with the original plan, but it also is useful to have some other options. By getting clients to think in this way, they attain a greater sense of possibility. They begin to see that there might be more than one way to achieve their objectives. Given the uncertainties of the labor market, having a back-up plan would seem to be a prudent undertaking in most situations.

Once the planning has been completed, it is important to put the plan on paper, in the language of the client. The general framework for this statement is as follows:

I, _____, am going to take a step toward achieving my

career goal of becoming a _____ by doing the following:

_____

_____

_____

_____

Signature: _____ Date: _____

Witnessed by: _____

While this has no legal ramifications, it does create a concrete document, and there is a greater likelihood that the plan will be taken seriously. Having the client and a witness sign the form helps to further communicate the importance of the plan that is being proposed. In an office setting, one copy of the plan should stay in the file and the other copy should be given to the client.

ADVOCACY AND SOCIAL ACTION

The process of action planning is one in which clients gain new understanding of their situation, make decisions, and engage in action steps to further their career goals. These action steps are designed as part of a process to generate broad-based career changes. From a systems perspective, one change in the system has the potential to impact many other areas.

In most situations, the underlying premise in action planning is that the responsibility for making change is one that rests with the client. The career counselor plays a supportive role in this process, but that is as far as it goes. There are many situations, however, where the counselor needs to expand the counseling role to include advocacy and social action. Sometimes the only way to implement effective change is through a more socially active stance.

One illustration involves developmentally disabled clients who require extra assistance to locate work and educational placements. This group of clients still must take action, but there are some actions that need to be taken on their behalf. Career counselors operating in this environment must assume a more active stance while at the same time being careful to not become too dominant. If counselors become too active, there is the danger of creating unnecessary dependence. It is a matter of balancing out what is really needed with the capacities of the clients who are being served.

In other situations, career counselors might become involved in local and national issues to help establish new and more enlightened social policies. This involvement can be achieved individually or through various associations. Career counselors have an important perspective to add to the political debate. Changes made at this level can reduce some of the barriers facing clients and counselors.

SUMMARY

This chapter has focused on the shift toward action planning. As a first step, there is the consolidation of information and the need to respect the pace at which the client is pulling information together. There also are shifts as clients move toward various educational or work-related options. These involve both intuitive and rational methods. In our complex and fast-paced society, there is a need for comprehensive decision-making methods that draw from both sides of the brain. Gelatt's (1989) framework of positive uncertainty seems well suited to the current situation.

It is not unusual, as people move toward action, for some forms of resistance to emerge. This resistance can be the result of clients and counselors moving at different speeds, there can be uncertainties and fears about making mistakes, and feelings of loss can emerge.

The action plan itself is something that needs to be concrete and specific. There may be a need for a referral. Also, given the complexity of our situation, it can be helpful to develop a back-up plan.

In most cases there is a focus on helping the client to develop new understanding and to assume responsibility for her actions. While this is generally very helpful, there also are situations where social action and advocacy need to be implemented. This two-pronged approach to counseling service helps to create a dynamic and effective career counseling practice.

Implementing
Action Plans

- **Providing Support to Clients**

- **Processing New Insights and Information**

- **Action Plans That Aren't Followed Through**

- **Handling Additional Concerns**

The notion of action planning is something that tends to get emphasized toward the end of the career counseling process. While this certainly is the case, it is also important to recognize that action planning flows through every aspect of counseling (Amundson, 1995). In some respects, the first contact with a counselor is the result of an action plan that is being implemented. During and between sessions there also are small action plans that help to set the shape of career counseling. Action planning is closely aligned with intentionality and human agency (Chen, 2006). It is an expression of personal attitudes and aptitudes and a way for people to generate change in their lives.

There is movement in the action planning process as time progresses. Goals are refined and plans are made to engage in some form of formal action plan. At times, this action moves clients to a new setting through referral or through enrollment in other programs. There also are shifts as clients move toward various educational or work-related options.

Borgen and Maglio (2007) recently completed an interesting research study focusing on the reflections of clients who had developed an action plan as part of an employment or career guidance program. In this qualitative interview-based study, people were encouraged to explore what helped and what hindered them in implementing the action plans that they had developed. On the positive side of the ledger, participants commented on how their personal attitudes, self-knowledge, and support from others contributed to their implementation of the action plan. They also mentioned flexibility, goal clarity, broader perspectives, and financial resources as important elements. The factors that hindered action planning at a personal level involved low levels of motivation, negative emotions, lack of experience, skill problems, and health issues. At a broader social level there were problems with the "system," counseling agencies, companies, discrimination, financial difficulties, and a general lack of support from others.

Undoubtedly there are many challenges associated with implementing an effective action plan. In this chapter we will explore ways in which career counselors can be supportive in this process.

PROVIDING SUPPORT TO CLIENTS

As clients attempt to implement their action plans, they often require ongoing emotional and practical support. The career counselor plays an important role during this implementation phase. One of the ways in which counselors offer support is by checking in with clients as they move forward. In some situations, clients are instructed to call the counselor or leave a message when they have completed a particular task. The counselor might also initiate some form of follow-up connection. One interesting and innovative example of this process was a career counselor who made three copies of the action plan: one for the client, one for the file, and the third copy to be mailed to the client a month afterward. Mailing the plan served as a nonjudgmental reminder of the original agreement.

One of the most challenging tasks for counselors is finding the time to do adequate follow-up. Given current workloads, many career counselors find themselves with insufficient time to properly undertake follow-up activities. This failure to follow up with clients has consequences for clients, but also impacts counselors. Follow-up serves as a useful way for counselors to get information about clients' progress and also to learn more about their effectiveness as counselors. This information can be encouraging and also instructive. Without follow-up, career counselors never get to appreciate the full impact of their efforts.

As counselors contemplate the need for support as part of action planning, it is often helpful to build this in as part of the action plan. This means asking some additional questions and organizing a way for clients to get support after they finish career counseling. The client may have family members or friends who can be utilized for this purpose. These other community resources can offer various forms of emotional and practical support. Actively setting up a structure for broad-based support can be an important part of the career counseling process.

Chapter 7 contained a discussion of how important it was to get input from family and friends during career counseling (Amundson & Penner, 1998). Through this process, there is an opportunity to connect with a variety of people who could play a significant role once formal action steps are being taken. Involvement of significant others can take many forms once counseling is completed. Burton and Wedemeyer (1991) describe the job search process as one in which the role of the job seeker is to be the CEO of Job Search. As part of Job Search, there is a need for a board of directors to provide encouragement and direction. These directors are consulted on a regular basis, and the job seeker must provide reports on how Job Search is progressing. While this type of formal structure may be beyond the scope of many people, there certainly is a need for some type of formal or informal support network. Research on the dynamics of unemployment suggests that support from family and friends is critical for people who are unemployed (Borgen & Amundson, 1987). Part of the problem, however, is that there is a natural tendency to withdraw at the time when support is most needed. Because of this dynamic, career counselors must organize support networks whenever possible.

Support for the client's action plan might also require additional work by the counselor. The development of an action plan does not necessarily mean that closure is close at hand. Sometimes career counselors must provide some practical skill support as part of the next step. A good example is a situation where clients need to learn job search skills. In many situations, this training would be available through short courses in the community. There are some situations, however, where this is not feasible. Under these conditions, the career counselor may need to build this skill training into the counseling process as part of the action plan. In some situations, this might mean offering some direct assistance with building a resume and developing a job search plan. In other instances it might require practice with interviewing skills. Whatever the need, the career counselor must be prepared to offer some practical assistance.

The degree of involvement in the practical skill training area can vary considerably, depending on what is needed. Sometimes it is merely a matter of orienting clients to the necessary books and training resources. At other times, more direct intervention is required. In one of our career training courses, one of the assignments is to find a "resume challenged" individual (a young person who has few skills; someone returning to work; someone changing work fields) and help him construct a resume. Initially the task seems straightforward. The end result, however, is often very surprising. In many respects the process becomes as important as the final result. Self-esteem is bolstered, people learn about transferable skills, and there usually is a renewed motivation for job finding. While it isn't possible to offer this type of service in every instance, it is something that can be beneficial in special situations.

Many clients have difficulty in answering behaviorally oriented interview questions. They might have a resume that outlines their educational and work skills, but employers are interested in many other skills. For example, an employer might want to know whether the person can work in a team. The best way to answer this type of question is usually with a story, a concrete illustration. Helping clients to find their good stories is an important part of the preparation process. As we have worked with this method, we have found that finding good stories is only the first step. Once the story has been identified, there is a process of assessing everything that has been communicated through the story. In one situation, the client, Dale, spoke about his eldership responsibilities as part of a church group. The example that was used clearly illustrated teamwork but the counselor pointed out that it also reflected leadership, empathy, persistence, creativity, courage, and hard work. The telling of the story is really a "value added" event. In addition to learning about teamwork, all other qualities become evident. Dale could use the same story (with minor modifications) to provide an illustration of leadership, empathy, persistence, and so on. Having a few good stories goes a long way toward preparing the person for an interview. Of course, identifying the story needs to be then followed with further learning about how best to tell the story. Many people get lost in the details and need practice in how to express themselves in a clear and concise manner. Again, this is something that can be done by a counselor or it can be part of a career development group.

PROCESSING NEW INSIGHTS AND INFORMATION

Many career counselors find themselves in a position where they are managing cases as well as providing direct career counseling. With this scenario, a sequence of action plans are anticipated. It is the career counselor's role to follow and manage the general flow of activities. Along the way new insights and information may emerge. The counselor needs to record this information and also debrief the process with clients. It sometimes leads to new interventions. As an illustration of this process, consider the following case scenario:

Background: Jane was excited about starting college but needed to make some money during the summer to help her with expenses. Through the career program at her school (taught by the counselor) she was able to develop a good resume. She made some contacts and even arranged some interviews (her action plan). Unfortunately, nothing seemed to be working and she was discouraged. She came to see the school counselor to see if there was anything else she should be doing.

Counselor	You sound pretty discouraged when you talk about looking for work.
Jane	I did so much preparation and nothing seems to be working. I don't know what I'm going to do if I can't land a decent job.
Counselor	It's very frustrating and it sounds as if you are feeling a real sense of desperation.
Jane	Yes! I so much want a job, maybe too much. I know that it ties me up when I go to interviews. I just feel that I can't really express myself. All I think about is "I wonder if they like me?"
Counselor	It seems that there are almost two conversations going on in your head when you try to answer questions in the interview.
Jane	Yeah. I keep wondering what they are thinking and doubting whether I can really do the job. I know from what we talked about in the career class that I am really shooting myself in the foot.
Counselor	What do you need to do to push that critical voice into the background?
Jane	I don't know, maybe doing some practice interviews might help.
Counselor	Is that something we could do together?
Jane	That would be great. I have just lost all my confidence.
Counselor	Let's see if we can set up an appointment for next week and try some interviewing.

(Note: During these practice sessions it would be important for the counselor to not only practice behavioral interviewing skills but to also use reflection to change some of the client's internal dialogue.)

You will notice in this counselor–client dialogue that the school counselor (who has career counseling skills) uses empathic reflection to understand the emotional as well as the cognitive and behavioral elements of the situation. Rather than moving too quickly to solve the problem, the counselor engages in collaborative problem solving. It is only after the client makes the suggestion that the counselor responds with an offer of service. Again, it is important to ensure a significant role for the client in any changes to the original action plan.

Sometimes, during this final phase, there can be some new information that requires a major rethinking of the career directions being contemplated. Career counselors need to be prepared to return to the exploration phase when information emerges that significantly changes the nature of the action planning. As an illustration, consider the case of Amanda. She was putting together the areas of fine arts and computers and looking into the field of graphic design. At one level, this sounded like the perfect solution—perhaps too perfect!

Amanda	I've had a chance to meet with some graphic designers and it looks like they have a lot of fun. I saw some of the work they were doing and it looked really interesting. But the more I found out about it, the more I realized that it wasn't for me. Did you know that most of them just work from project to project? It's really feast or famine. I don't think that I could live like that.
Counselor	It sounds as if these interviews were really helpful for you, at least you now know what you don't want.
Amanda	Yeah, I need a lot more security in my life. I want a job that isn't quite so uncertain.
Counselor	Maybe you could tell me more about what types of firms that you visited.
Amanda	I had a friend who knew about a small graphic design company that was just starting up in our area. I met with them and then with another graphic designer who works as an independent contractor.
Counselor	I wonder if you really have surveyed the complete field of graphic design? The people you were interviewing were all operating from more of an entrepreneurial base. Do you think that you might be able to find others who would be working in a different organizational structure?
Amanda	Well, I guess I could keep meeting with people.
Counselor	You don't sound too convinced. How would you like to continue?
Amanda	I just don't know where else to look. These were all the names I had.
Counselor	Do you think it would be worthwhile to see what we could come up with on the Internet?
Amanda	Sure, that would be OK.

(*Counselor and client work together on the Internet. During the search, they discover a graphic designer association and a large firm in their community that seems to employ graphic designers.*)

Counselor	Do you feel OK contacting the firm and the association?
Amanda	Sure.
Counselor	When do you think you will be making the contact? I'd like to hear how it goes.
Amanda	Well, I could make the calls this afternoon and call you later in the day.
Counselor	That would be great. I really would like to know.
Amanda	Maybe after I call you we can make another appointment.
Counselor	That would be fine.

In this scenario, the client is ready to change focus when perhaps all that is needed is more research and more careful planning about the conditions of employment. The career counselor engages in collaborative problem solving and expresses a genuine interest in the outcome of the further exploration. This sets the stage for the next appointment.

ACTION PLANS THAT AREN'T FOLLOWED THROUGH

Despite all the care and attention that goes into action planning, there are times when clients don't follow through with the plans that have been generated. Without a good follow-up system, this type of inaction is often missed. By following up with clients, counselors have the opportunity to hear about the successes and also the times when nothing really happens. Naturally, it is disappointing when little has been done with respect to the action plan. Rather than assigning blame for the lack of action, however, it is more helpful to use this as a learning opportunity for both the client and the counselor. Clients should be encouraged to return for career counseling with the objective of working out a new plan of action.

As a starting point for this type of counselor–client interaction, it is important to maintain the relationship by being nonjudgmental, genuine, and empathic. There is little to be gained by finding fault in the other person. What does need to happen is a brief exploration of the situation and some further collaborative problem solving. To illustrate this process, consider the following dialogue:

George	I just never had a chance to make those phone calls that we talked about. I was so busy with other things last week.
Counselor	When you left, you seemed excited about some of the information interviewing you were going to try. I wonder if we can capture that excitement again, but set it up differently so that you will find ways to fit it into your schedule? (Note: You will notice that the counselor doesn't get into a discussion of the excuses that are being made. The focus is on what didn't happen and the need to try again with a new plan.)
George	I'm still really interested in making those calls. Without that information I can't really take the next step.
Counselor	So what needs to happen, George, to make sure that you can make the calls?
George	I don't know, I'm not too sure that I know exactly what to say.
Counselor	Maybe we need to do a few practice runs before you make the calls?
George	That would be really helpful. Could we meet later this week? I really need to get on with these calls.

In this situation the client, George, is finding ways to avoid the action plan because he lacks confidence in his ability to speak on the telephone. By adding an additional step (interview practice) there is a greater likelihood of the plan being carried through. Sometimes, the best way forward is to break the action plan down into smaller pieces and add some additional steps. These steps can build self-confidence and also provide some additional skill development. The goal is to create plans of action that are both realistic and attainable.

There are also those situations where the action plan really belongs mainly to the counselor and not to the client. In these instances, the counselor has moved too quickly. While the plan might be a good one, without client "buy-in" there is little chance that much will be accomplished. Often, the key indicator is body language. Clients may be saying one thing verbally, but the body language might be inconsistent with what is being expressed. Consider the following situation:

Maggie	I haven't been able to find any information about the program.
Counselor	You don't sound very enthusiastic about looking for the information. Earlier you said that you wanted to learn more about opportunities in dentistry. You certainly have a good academic record.
Maggie	I guess dentistry will be OK.
Counselor	I wonder if we need to look more closely at this. Maybe we are moving too quickly here.
Maggie	My parents said it would be a good career for me.
Counselor	But it sounds as if you're not too sure about it.
Maggie	Yeah, I want to make them happy, but I wonder if this is enough.
Counselor	Let's talk more about how you are feeling and some of your ideas.

In this scenario, the career counselor noticed the lack of enthusiasm and reflected this back to Maggie. This empathic reflection helped set the stage for a new discussion about the differences between her wishes and those of her parents. Sometimes, when counselors get too busy, they miss some of the important underlying clues. In this instance, the counselor noticed what was happening and was willing to engage in further discussion about Maggie's feelings and ideas.

The examples we have been discussing thus far are pretty straightforward, and there is a good likelihood of resolution. There also are more difficult situations, particularly when clients repeatedly fail to follow through with action plans. While some rebuilding of action plans is justifiable, after a while the discussion needs to reflect this process. The discussion might proceed as follows:

Counselor	I wonder what is happening here. This is our third action planning meeting and it seems that not much progress is being made.
Jonathan	I am just too busy right now to carry this forward.
Counselor	I know that you are busy, but I am wondering if there is more to it?

| Jonathan | No, it's just the busyness. |
| Counselor | Maybe it would be helpful to take a break and come back to this when you have more time. |

There certainly is little point in continuing with action planning efforts if the client is not following through. In this scenario, action planning would only resume after a break, and then it might involve a referral or a change in structure, so that there would be a greater likelihood of completion.

Metaphors can also be used as a way to represent some of the lack of progression that might be happening. Suppose that the problem is viewed within the context of "climbing a mountain." In this process there certainly is not a linear pathway. At times movement is forward, but there also are moments when people need to retrace their steps and try again from a different perspective. In serious mountain climbing there are also instances when people need to build a "base camp" from which to operate. There are stoppages in the journey and moments when people need to rebuild their strength before continuing. Using this framework, clients can view their lack of movement in a more positive perspective. Rather than being a failure, the lack of action might just be a time to reflect, rebuild, and seek new ways of continuing.

HANDLING ADDITIONAL CONCERNS

As clients complete their action plans, there may be other issues that need to be addressed. For many people, career counseling is a process requiring the development of multiple action plans. There is a need to build on successes and to use what has been accomplished for further exploration and action planning.

When clients first present their problems, they may have many issues that could be addressed. Rather than trying to do everything at once, the counselor must isolate the issues and deal with them one at a time. For example, a client may have issues that cross over several employability domains. They may have done little self-reflection and as a result they might have few ideas about career possibilities. In addition, they may need to explore training options and look for a part-time job to support their educational efforts. All of these tasks can be overwhelming—for the client as well as for the counselor. By taking them one at a time, there is a better opportunity to generate momentum and to realize long-term success.

Career counselors should be prepared for issues to shift as the process proceeds. A small change in one area can have an impact on other areas of concern. For example, while the issues just described are different in nature, there is little doubt that self-confidence plays an important part in each employability domain. If people acquire a greater sense of self-confidence through the self-exploration process, they will be better prepared to explore educational training and to undertake a more effective job search.

SUMMARY

In this chapter, we have examined the ways in which action plans are implemented, including the key role of ongoing counselor support. This support can be both emotional (encouragement) and practical (skill development). Career counselors need to follow through with clients to ensure that they have the necessary resources to successfully complete the action plans that have been developed.

As part of action planning, it is not uncommon to have new information and insights emerge. This creates additional opportunities for discussion, flexibility, and for making adjustments to the original action plan. With counselor support and a collaborative problem-solving process, there is a greater likelihood of long-term success.

There are always those situations in which action plans are not successfully implemented. While this can be disappointing, it also presents an opportunity for further learning. Perhaps the plan was too complex or maybe more basic skill development was needed. Another possibility is that counselors get ahead of their clients in trying to formulate appropriate actions. Whatever the cause, there is a need to be nonjudgmental and to return to the exploration phase.

Career counselors should help clients manage the general flow of action plans. Many clients need to complete a series of action plans in order to arrive at their goals. Each action plan represents part of a foundation that sets the stage for long-term success.

Evaluating Client Progress

- **Evaluating Client Progress During the Course of Career Counseling**

- **Evaluating Client Progress at the End of Career Counseling**

In any type of counseling, evaluating client progress toward goal achievement is essential to providing helpful assistance. This is especially true in career counseling, because it is often a brief experience and the goals that clients express during intake often change substantially over the course of counseling (Niles et al., 2000). Connecting client goals to the evaluation process is important because goals serve as the guideposts for directing career counseling activities. Goals also provide the focal points for evaluating the effectiveness of career counseling. When the career counselor and the client discuss the progress the client is making, they do so in light of the goals they have established. Goal setting and evaluating client progress are two career counseling activities that are closely linked.

From the onset, note an important point related to evaluating client progress: Evaluation can often be viewed negatively. That is, some people view evaluation as an activity in which one person is judged according to whether they have done "what they were supposed to do." This can be true for the client and the career counselor. For example, a beginning career counselor can feel threatened by the prospect of exploring how well career counseling is going, because he is unsure of his competency level and afraid that the evaluation could reveal his shortcomings as a career counselor. The client could worry that she is not making sufficient progress and that evaluation will point out her "failings" in this regard. When viewed from this perspective, evaluation becomes threatening and heightens the defensiveness of the participants. This is not how we view evaluation in career counseling. Rather, we consider evaluating career counseling as an opportunity to provide important information to clients regarding the progress they have made and the progress that might be useful for them to make as they move forward. It also offers the participants the opportunity to identify which interventions are most helpful and what issues need to be addressed as career counseling proceeds. This assessment is performed collaboratively, with both participants (i.e., the counselor and client) engaging in an honest and sensitive discussion about their perceptions regarding the client's progress. Thus, this sort of evaluation is developmental. If the client's career development is "stuck," it is important to understand what obstacles are preventing the client from moving forward and what the counselor might need to do to help the client become "unstuck." Evaluation, therefore, requires the career counselor to use the same sort of skills (e.g., empathy, immediacy, genuineness, and congruency) necessary for developing and maintaining an effective working alliance with the client. To engage in this sort of evaluation, the career counselor must develop a sense of comfort relative to evaluation. If the career counselor experiences uneasiness about this process, then she should discuss this with her supervisor prior to engaging in the evaluation process. It will be hard, if not impossible, for the career counselor to provide a safe environment for evaluation if the counselor himself does not feel comfortable with this process.

Evaluation also suggests that the career counselor and client incorporate data to compare client's progress to client's goals. These data can be empirical, opinion, and/or behavioral in nature. Evaluation can incorporate empirical data in the form of precounseling and postcounseling comparisons. For example, a career counselor might share with the client the following: "When we compare your scores on the decision scale from when you started career counseling until today, you have decreased your career indecision by 10 points. This suggests you have become much more decided in your career choice. How do you see it?"

Evaluation can also include the opinions of the counselor and client based on their perceptions of the career counseling process. For instance, the career counselor might share the following: "I get the sense that you have worked hard to increase your self-understanding in important areas. You have worked hard to clarify your values and you seem to be clear about what is important to you now. How do you see it?" After discussing this with the client, the career counselor could inquire as to what topics the client feels would be most helpful to explore next in their work together.

Evaluating client progress can also involve behavioral data related to the client's activities (how many resumes the client has circulated, how many contacts the client has made for information interviews, how many self-assessment exercises the client has completed, and so on). Consider the following career counselor statement: "You have made one information interviewing contact so far. We had set a goal of making 3–5 contacts per week for the next three weeks. It may be useful for us to discuss what your experiences has been thus far regarding making contacts for information interviewing." In this case, there may be the need to reduce the target goal of conducting 3–5 contacts per week if the client now views this as unattainable. Thus, evaluation can incorporate outcome data, opinion data, and/or behavioral data. In each instance, the data discussed when providing feedback to the client should be connected to the client's goals for career counseling.

Although an obvious time for the career counselor and client to engage in evaluating client progress toward goal achievement is at the end of career counseling, we think that evaluating client progress is important throughout the career counseling process. We will first discuss evaluating client progress during the course of career counseling. Then, we will discuss evaluating client progress at the end, or termination stage, of career counseling.

EVALUATING CLIENT PROGRESS DURING THE COURSE OF CAREER COUNSELING

Evaluating client progress during the course of career counseling is important for several reasons. First, it provides the counselor and client with the opportunity to discuss whether the career counseling activities are "on target" and useful. This sort of discussion actively engages the client in the career counseling intervention process. The client experiences a sense of ownership in, and responsibility for, the career counseling process. It also ensures that the career counselor is incorporating the client's perspective and context into the career counseling experience. Functioning from the client's perspective and context is a key tenet for effective multicultural career counseling (Leong, 1996). Thus, engaging the client in a collaborative discussion related to the career counseling process fosters a sense of honoring the client's cultural context and experiences. It is empowering to the client and provides the opportunity to fit the career counseling interventions to the client, rather than vice versa.

CAREER COUNSELING GOALS OFTEN CHANGE OVER TIME

Evaluating progress during the course of career counseling is also important because it is common for the client's goals to change as career counseling evolves. The client's goals often shift in career counseling because career concerns merge with issues such as past and present relationship concerns and a variety of nonwork issues such as inter-role conflict (Anderson & Niles, 1995). As career counseling evolves, many clients expand their goals to include their nonwork issues within the career decision-making process. As Super, Savickas, and Super (1996) have noted, while people are busy making a living, they are also busy living a life. Career counseling, with adults in particular, tends to reflect this reality over time.

However, it is common that, at the onset of career counseling, clients do not recognize the overlap that exists between work and nonwork issues. Thus, they may attempt to make their concerns conform to the common notion that creates a false dichotomy between career and personal issues. This is not surprising, because many of our career counseling models reinforce this artificial dichotomy (Niles & Harris-Bowlsbey, 2005). In instances in which the content of career counseling reflects the overlap between work and nonwork issues, but the client's goals do not, the career counselor can explore whether the client desires to revise the goals for career counseling. Career counselors can invite clients to consider this sort of goal revision by providing a psychoeducational perspective to help clients understand that the activity of examining career concerns within a life context is normal and often more realistic than trying to address career concerns in an isolated fashion. Counselors can help clients understand this by providing statements such as the following: "Often, people seem to think that nonwork issues should be kept out of the career counseling process. However, my experience has been that, when these issues are brought into career counseling, people are able to consider their career concerns in ways that more accurately reflect how they live their lives. When this happens, career counseling can be more useful because it more closely resembles life as people live it." Offering this invitation gives clients permission to engage in a more holistic career counseling experience.

Career counselors can use immediacy skills to encourage clients when there is an incongruity between the client's goals and the career counseling content. For example, counselors can offer statements such as the following: "I've noticed that we have been focusing on how your career decisions may impact your family situation. Would you like to revise your goals to include this concern?"

Clients can experience shifting career counseling goals for other reasons as well. For example, some clients may experience frustrating work situations that lead them to seek career counseling. Their initial interest in receiving career assistance may be to find a new job. However, after having the opportunity to express their emotional dissatisfaction to an empathic career counselor, it may be that the client decides he can tolerate the current situation by focusing on acquiring new coping skills such as assertiveness, cognitive coping skills, and stress management strategies.

There are numerous reasons why career counselors need to evaluate client progress during the course of career counseling. The main point in this section of the chapter is that, because career counseling goals are intertwined with evaluating client progress, career counselors must demonstrate flexibility when addressing their client's emerging goals. Although goals expressed at intake provide useful starting points for the initial focus of career counseling, as counselors note shifts in the client's concerns expressed in career counseling, they should explore (with their clients) whether the emerging concerns have implications for the relevance of the established career counseling goals. By paying attention to the pattern of client concerns and staying mindful of the degree to which they relate to the client's established goals, career counselors will increase the likelihood that their interventions will address their client's needs throughout the course of career counseling.

CAREER COUNSELING IS OFTEN SHORT-TERM COUNSELING

Career counseling tends to be short-term counseling. Thus, there is a degree to which efficiency is essential to making the most of the limited time the career counselor and client have together. Career counseling efficiency is only useful when it includes addressing the client's career concerns effectively and thereby helps the client achieve his or her goals. Therefore, career counselors should begin addressing the importance of evaluating client progress toward goal achievement in the initial career counseling session.

Some career counselors also take the approach of establishing a time to evaluate client progress rather early in the career counseling relationship. For example, a career counselor might suggest the following: "We can meet for up to ten sessions, however, I recommend that we meet for three sessions and then discuss whether you are finding our work together useful for you. If you are, then we can continue. If not, then we can discuss what we need to do differently to make the experience more helpful to you. Or, if you decide to terminate at that time, we could discuss that as well. How does that sound to you?"

This approach establishes an agreed-upon time when the counselor and client can evaluate the career counseling experience. This approach provides an established point in the career counseling relationship, when the client and counselor know that the process will be discussed and career counseling progress will be reviewed. This time can also be used to clarify the goals that will guide the content of subsequent career counseling sessions. Taking this approach is also useful, because clients may be reluctant to commit to greater than a few sessions at the onset of career counseling but often find it desirable to continue once they have reached the three-session point. The following provides an example of how the career counselor can evaluate client progress in the third session:

Counselor   This is our third session and we agreed in our first meeting that we would use this session to discuss how you feel about

	our work together and whether you think it will be useful to you for us to continue our work together.
Client	Yes, I remember.
Counselor	Great, so tell me how you are feeling about our work together thus far.
Client	I think we are off to a good start. I know at the beginning you mentioned that career counseling often involves nonwork concerns and I wasn't sure I wanted to look at things other than my job. But now I am beginning to get a sense of how it may be helpful to me to look at how my choice of work fits with my other activities—like the time I have available for my kids. My last job required a lot of travel and I was away from home a lot. I want to be there for my kids, so I definitely want to cut down on that. I also would like to have some time to develop some hobbies. In my last job, I felt like all I did was work and I don't think that is a very healthy lifestyle.
Counselor	It sounds like we have a number of important topics to discuss together. Let me be sure I have what you have said thus far. You would like to continue working together. You also are interested in examining how you can design a career that allows you to have time to also experience other aspects of your life that are important to you like parenting and leisure.
Client	Yes, that's it. I realize that is a little different from what I said in my first session. Is it really okay for us to look at all these things in career counseling?
Counselor	Yes, in fact, I think it is a good idea to examine your career decisions in light of the sort of life you hope to construct for yourself. How about if we proceed with these goals in mind? We can meet together for another five sessions and then check in with each other again to see how you are experiencing our work together.
Client	Great.
Counselor	Sounds like we have a plan. But, before we proceed, let me be clear that if at anytime you would like to discuss our work together, I invite you to do so. I want this experience to be as meaningful to you as possible.
Client	I appreciate that.

Evaluating client progress during the course of career counseling contributes to maximizing career counselor and client time together. It provides opportunities to take corrective action when session content is not connected to client goals. Such an approach fits the career counseling experience to the client's concerns rather than trying to fit the client to a career counseling approach that might not address the client's situation as effectively.

EVALUATING CLIENT PROGRESS AT THE END OF CAREER COUNSELING

The ending, or termination stage, of career counseling is a distinct phase in the career counseling process. Termination is an obvious time to evaluate client progress. When handled effectively, termination provides the opportunity to bring closure to the career counseling relationship, reinforce client's gains/learning, and point out potential challenges that the client may encounter. Handling evaluation at termination requires the career counselor to prepare the client for this activity within the context of the relationship ending. Among other things, this requires the career counselor to eliminate any ambiguity regarding the fact that the relationship is ending, ensure that the evaluation process is sensitive to emotions related to the ending of the relationship, and provide a positive climate for evaluating client progress at termination.

ELIMINATE THE AMBIGUITY

For evaluation to be effective at termination, the termination should not be a surprise experience for the client. Career counselors begin preparing clients for termination in the initial session. If the career counseling is time limited, this is accomplished by making sure the client knows how many sessions are possible. The career counselor can provide a sort of "countdown" for clients as termination approaches. For example, career counselors can remind the client that, "There are three sessions left," then, "This is our next to last session together," and lastly, "As you know, this is our final session." A countdown approach ensures that there is no ambiguity about the end of career counseling. Eliminating ambiguity regarding termination is essential to providing an effective ending. When it is clear that the relationship is terminating, the career counselor provides an opportunity for the client to engage in a positive termination experience. Because endings can be bittersweet, they can involve a variety of emotions, including anger, sadness, excitement, hope, and disappointment. It is important that the client has the opportunity to express emotions he feels. Doing so creates the opportunity for the career counselor to validate the client's emotional experience. It is a chance for the client to feel his emotions regarding termination and learn that he can "live to tell about it." When clients are prepared for termination, they become active participants in the ending. They can say what they feel, be clear about what they experience, and learn to cope effectively with challenging emotions.

ADDRESSING THE EMOTIONS ASSOCIATED WITH ENDING

It is important for career counselors to be aware of the fact that termination can be difficult for both the career counselor and the client. Endings can be emotionally painful, and we often struggle with unresolved issues around endings in our lives (e.g., feelings of abandonment). For example, if we were not prepared for an ending, we are often left with "things unsaid." Or, we might not fully understand when a particular ending is occurring. In such instances, it often feels like the ending is something that happened to us rather than something in which we were participants. In such instances, unresolved grief work can enter into the career counseling experience and detract from the evaluation process at termination. For career counselors, these unresolved issues could enter into career counseling when they lack self-awareness regarding these previous life experiences involving difficult endings. For example, if the career counselor has had difficulty expressing feelings about loss related to relationships ending, the likelihood increases that the career counselor will minimize the ending of the career counseling relationship. At best, this dilutes the potential positive impact of the termination process for the client. Paying attention to a reluctance to engage the client in discussions related to termination provides the career counselor with an indication that counter-transference is influencing counselor behavior. Career counselors should discuss this experience with a colleague and/or supervisor. At times, career counselors will need to enter counseling to work through their own issues related to relationships terminating.

CREATING AN ENVIRONMENT FOR A POSITIVE ENDING

When termination is treated as it should be—as an important stage in career counseling—the evaluation process provides the client with a tremendous opportunity for self-growth and reinforces the acquisition of career self-management skills. Termination is the time when the career counselor and client review the client's progress, reinforce the skills learned and insights gained in career counseling, and identify potential challenges the client may encounter in the near future. In the former situation, the career counselor can encourage the client to discuss the actions taken to foster their career development. Emphasizing the initiative the client took to manage her career concerns is important. Noting the skills the client used to enhance self-understanding, explore career options, make career decisions, and seek job opportunities helps her clarify the skills she gained and actions she took to manage her career development. Because these skills will undoubtedly be needed in the future when the client encounters subsequent career dilemmas, it is important that the counselor and client review the steps the client took during career counseling. The career counselor and client can also discuss strategies the client can take to cope with future challenges. The following provides an example of a positive termination experience in career counseling:

Counselor	As I mentioned last week, this is our final session. I am wondering if you have any thoughts and/or feelings about that.
Client	I guess what I realize is that I will miss our meeting together to discuss my career concerns, so I feel a little sad about ending.
Counselor	I will miss our meeting together also. You have worked hard to advance in your career. Can you say some more about how you have found our meetings useful?

Client	Sure. I have appreciated your support as I have considered various options. It was nice to have the chance to talk about whatever I thought might be worth considering and I feel that you weren't judging me like some of my family members do when I mention my ideas to them. At first, I was surprised when we talked about some of my relationships because I didn't think that was done in career counseling. Now, however, I see how talking about ways in which my career decisions connect with other areas of my life is very important to helping me make good career decisions.
Counselor	I am pleased that you felt supported by me. I do support your thoughts and efforts. I think you have wisely been willing to explore your career development from a broad perspective. You have considered your career concerns from the context of your life experience. This will help you as you encounter challenges related to implementing your career plans.
Client	I think I have a better understanding of how to make good career decisions now than I did before we started working together, and that will help me too.
Counselor	Say some more about the difference between what you know about career decision-making now that you didn't know before career counseling.
Client	Now I know that I need to base a decision on who I am and what my life situation is. By that I mean that a good career decision starts with accurate self-understanding. I also understand that my work decisions influence my other life activities and vice versa.
Counselor	And, you have worked very hard to develop a solid foundation of self-understanding. As a result, you now seem to be much clearer about your values, skills, and interests.
Client	I also like what you said a few sessions ago, about how it is important to continue working at being self-aware. I am planning on continuing with your suggestion to keep a career awareness journal.
Counselor	You have done a great job with the journaling and that seems to have been very useful to you already with regard to developing important insights. I'm glad to hear that you are planning to continue with that.
Client	I appreciate the help you have given me.
Counselor	I have enjoyed working with you and I wish you the best as you continue moving forward. Feel free to call on me if I can be of any assistance to you in the future.
Client	Thank you. I will.

Addressing termination clearly and directly increases the chance that termination will be a positive experience for the client. Eliminating ambiguity regarding the ending contributes to this. Reinforcing client advances and being empathic toward client struggles provide the sort of atmosphere that is conducive to a positive ending.

Client	I remember that today is our last session.
Counselor	That's right, and one of the things for us to accomplish today is to talk about how you have progressed in the time we have worked together.
Client	I remember that we talked about doing this today when we met the last time. So, I have been thinking a bit about it. I am not exactly sure if I have done that well. I realize that there are some ways in which I have made some good progress, but maybe there are some ways in which I haven't.
Counselor	Talk to me about the ways in which you have made progress.
Client	Well, I know that I seem to be doing a better job with information interviewing.
Counselor	You have worked hard to identify potential job leads. You have also been willing to make numerous contacts in your job search. Although this was very intimidating to you initially, you have made substantial gains in this area. As a result, you now have some clear job opportunities. How does that feel to you?
Client	It feels good, especially because this is something that didn't come easily to me. I am so introverted that the idea of networking sounded as challenging to me, at first, as climbing Mt. Everest! Even though I might not be the greatest at it now, it is something I can do and I realize that it is important for me to do this to get a job after I graduate from technical school.
Counselor	I'm wondering what you think are the important skills you have learned in the area of information interviewing.
Client	Well, one of the big ones is to always come away from the interview with another name or with several other names of people who I can contact for additional interviews. I also think an important skill relates to just having the right attitude about information interviews.
Counselor	Can you say more about this?
Client	Well, it connects to one of the challenges I had at the beginning of career counseling. I can be afraid to talk to people I don't know, and that is especially true when I feel like I am asking them for a favor.
Counselor	What has helped you to deal with this?
Client	I think it has helped me to remember that most people enjoy talking about themselves and their lives. It also helps when I know somebody that they know. Keeping these two things in mind has helped a lot.

| Counselor | It will be important for you to remind yourself of that when you do information interviewing in the future. |
| Client | That's right. |

The counselor and client have worked to identify gains made, identify struggles encountered, and note the strategies the client used to overcome those struggles. The career counselor reinforced this and reminded the client that those strategies are likely to be useful in the future. In situations in which it is possible for the career counselor to be of assistance to the client in the future, it is helpful (and often reassuring) to the client if the counselor mentions this possibility in the termination session.

| Counselor | Even though we are ending our work today, if you need help in the future, please feel free to contact me. |
| Client | Thank you very much. I will keep that in mind. |

Noting that the experience has been positive (if, in fact, it has!) is also appropriate during termination. Expressing feelings can help bring closure to the relationship and reinforce the fact that acknowledging feelings is a healing activity.

| Counselor | I have enjoyed working with you and will miss our work together. I think that our working together has been a positive experience. I think we made a good team. I am very pleased for you that you have worked so hard to manage your career development. That approach will help you to manage your career in the future. I wish you the best. |
| Client | Thank you. I have also enjoyed our work together. I appreciate the help you have given me. |

KNOWING WHEN TO TERMINATE

The decision to terminate or end career counseling can occur for several reasons. The most obvious reason to end career counseling is that the client has achieved his goals. This usually involves the client having a clear sense of direction regarding next steps. In some cases, it may even involve the client having implemented his plans and adjusted effectively to his new situation. In these situations, it becomes obvious that ending career counseling is appropriate.

In many instances, however, there is no such clear and obvious point reached in career counseling. A client may decide, for example, that due to various constraints (finances or family obligations) taking immediate action is not possible. In these instances, a client may terminate career counseling with a future plan that will be implemented once the current restrictions no longer exist. Reviewing the client's progress and supporting the client's decision become useful in these situations.

Sometimes, career counseling does not involve such natural endings. Career counselors may be restricted to the number of sessions they can provide and, therefore, the relationship can terminate before the client's goals are achieved. This can occur, for example, in practicum and internship experiences or in career counseling centers with limited counselor resources. Evaluating progress in these instances also includes a discussion about what additional resources the client can access to continue moving forward in her career development. For example, resources such as information interviewing contacts, job shadowing possibilities, and other career counselors with whom the client can work may be some relevant options.

SUMMARY

Evaluating client progress is essential throughout career counseling. Evaluation during the course of career counseling provides the opportunity to actively engage the client in the career counseling process and increases the probability that career counseling will be useful to the client. Evaluating client progress at the end of career counseling provides the opportunity to reinforce client's gains made in the career counseling process and to identify a plan of action once career counseling ends. In all instances, evaluating client progress is most effective when it is a collaborative process that connects to the client's goals. Being sensitive to client apprehensiveness related to evaluation (i.e., feeling that they are being judged) and being aware of one's own issues with evaluation are important keys to increasing the effectiveness of evaluation.

CHAPTER

Adapting Career Counseling to Counseling Settings

- **School Settings**
- **University Settings**
- **Community Settings**

Thus far, we have described career counseling without concern for the specific settings in which it occurs. Clearly, career counseling occurs in most settings in which counselors work. The standards of the American School Counselor Association (ASCA) (Campbell & Dahir, 1997), for example, include career development as one of the three primary areas of work for school counselors. The standards of the Council for the Accreditation of Counseling and Related Educational Programs (CACREP, 2009) include career development as a core area required in all counselor training programs at the master's and doctoral levels. College student surveys consistently reveal that students' concerns focus on the need for career planning assistance (Herr, Cramer, & Niles, 2004). Adults realize that the concept of a "permanent" job is passé and, therefore, the need exists to learn the requisite skills for engaging in effective career self-management. Counselors will, undoubtedly, encounter clients who have career concerns regardless of their work settings. Corporate employers understand that keeping employees satisfied in their career development increases productivity and maximizes the use of human capital in the workplace. Military personnel understand the importance of helping those in the armed forces transition smoothly to the civilian workforce. Moreover, part of an effectively functioning military includes helping those in the armed services work in military occupational specialties for which they are competent and interested.

It is just as clear that counselors will need to adapt the generic career counseling processes and procedures we have provided in this book to their own particular settings. In fact, there may be just as much variability within settings (i.e., schools, universities, community agencies) regarding how career counseling is practiced as there is across settings. For example, in some university career centers, career "counseling" resembles career advising more than a counseling-based intervention. Some high school counselors balance group career interventions with limited individual career planning assistance, while others may only offer individual assistance if an individual student requests it. Some community agencies may ignore career interventions completely, and others may have a practitioner who specializes in career services. Other agencies may have a list of career practitioners they use as referral services for clients who have career concerns. Employment agencies may have career counselors who have the appropriate training and credentials, or they may have people who have limited training in providing career advice. Private practitioners providing career assistance in some states must have counselor training, experience, and a professional counseling license to provide career counseling. In other states, people who do not have credentials and training can provide career assistance. There are, therefore, interactions among the counselor's personal theory of career counseling, the level of counselor training, the client's needs, and how career assistance is provided within the specific setting in which the counselor works. We have written this book with the primary goal of helping career counselors function more effectively in their professional practice of career counseling. We think practicing career counseling ethically requires people to have at least a master's degree in counseling or a related field, specific coursework in career development interventions, supervised career counseling practice, and the appropriate counseling credentials. Even with these requirements, however, we realize that the professional practice of career counseling will vary among and within school, university, workplace, and community settings. We also know that career practitioners who have less education than a master's degree can be important resources for activities such as accessing career information and learning about job search skills.

The NCDA recently created career practitioner designations that provide consumers with an initial description of a career counselor's level of expertise. For example, the Master Career Counselor (MCC) designation is awarded to a professional career counselor who holds a master's degree in counseling or related field and has been active as an NCDA member for a minimum of two years. Specifically, an MCC has at least three years of post-master's experience in career counseling and holds the credential of nationally certified counselor (NCC), licensed professional counselor (LPC), and/or licensed psychologist. MCCs must have successfully completed at least three credits of coursework in each of the six NCDA competency areas and must have completed a supervised career counseling practicum or two years of supervised career counseling work experience under a certified supervisor or an LPC. MCCs are skilled in administering and interpreting career assessments and provide the highest quality of career counseling services.

The NCDA notes the following with regard to the services provided by MCCs (www.ncda.org):

> . . . MCCs, or other professional career counselors, help people make decisions and plans related to life/career directions. The strategies and techniques are tailored to the specific needs of the person seeking help. It is likely that the career counselor will do one or more of the following:
> > Conduct individual and group personal counseling sessions to help clarify life/ career goals.
> > Administer and interpret tests and inventories to assess abilities, interests, and so forth, and to identify career options.
> > Encourage exploratory activities through assignments and planning experiences.
> > Utilize career planning systems and occupational information systems to help individuals better understand the world of work.
> > Provide opportunities for improving decision making skills.
> > Assist in developing individualized career plans.
> > Teach job hunting strategies and skills and assist in the development of resumes.
> > Help resolve potential personal conflicts on the job through practice in human relations skills.
> > Assist in understanding the integration of work and other life roles.
> > Provide support for persons experiencing job stress, job loss, and/or career transition.

The NCDA also created the designation of Master Career Development Professional (MCDP). The MCDP designation is designed to recognize experienced career development professionals who provide specialized career development services. MCDPs may include career development facilitators, career technicians, resume writers, employment agency professionals, career coaches, career management professionals, and workforce development professionals. The degrees, licenses, and levels of supervision of these professionals may vary. The MCC and MCDP designations provide useful information to consumers concerning the experience, academic backgrounds, and range of services provided by career professionals. Career professionals who have MCC or MCDP designations practice in school, university, and community settings.

SCHOOL SETTINGS

As noted, the ASCA standards indicate that school counselors provide developmentally appropriate career assistance to students across all grade levels. Typically, elementary school students receive career assistance in the form of classroom guidance activities and field trips that seek to increase the student's self- and career awareness. The primary aims are to encourage students to develop a sense of self, to expose them to a wide variety of occupations, and to help them avoid engaging in premature foreclosure of educational and occupational options. Key to providing appropriate career assistance at this level is having an awareness and understanding of students' developmental processes and how general development may interact with career development. For example, Gottfredson (1996) has noted that as elementary school students become oriented to the world, they often eliminate occupational options from further consideration based on perceived gender appropriateness and socioeconomic class. Knowing that elementary school students are vulnerable to this influence guides elementary school counselors in constructing career interventions that seek to counterbalance such societal influences (such as providing students with examples of nontraditional workers in gender-stereotyped occupations). Such interventions are especially important for students who tend to experience the greatest amount of discriminatory treatment in society (i.e., students of color and females). Thus, career interventions at the elementary school level enhance the acquisition of accurate self- and occupational information. Engaging students in discussions in which they share their interests also provides opportunities for self-clarification. Exposing students to new activities and guiding their participation in them (e.g., music, art, scouting) fosters self-efficacy and fundamental exploratory behaviors, and supports curiosity—all important behaviors for exploration-stage tasks that students will confront in middle school. Classroom guidance and small group activities serve as excellent service-delivery modes for career interventions at the elementary school level.

Middle school students engage in exploratory activities to prepare for the educational and career planning activities they will experience in high school. Exploratory activities are grounded in the continued acquisition of accurate self- and occupational information. For example, structured opportunities to clarify interests (e.g., via administering interest inventories) provide useful information for guided learning about specific occupations. Computer-assisted career guidance systems (CACGS) also serve as a resource for educating students about themselves and how self-information relates to educational and career options. Of course, the benefits of having students use such systems are strongest when they are used in conjunction with counselor contact. CACGS can be integrated into counseling via individual and/or small group counseling interventions.

Extracurricular and cocurricular school activities also provide opportunities for learning more about oneself relative to interests and competencies. Such activities serve as a vehicle for developing the interpersonal skills essential for successful performance in work. During high school, students can be exposed to experiences that more closely approximate real-world work experiences (e.g., internships, part-time work, volunteer activities, externships). Additional self-assessment activities (provided either individually or in groups) and guided career and educational exploration activities help high school students advance in their careers. These brief examples illustrate how career counseling theories interact with student needs in specific settings to influence the manner of service delivery required to meet the need. When school counselors have student-to-counselor ratios that often exceed 500:1, the need exists to provide career counseling that is brief and that involves multiple students simultaneously.

Most likely, school counselors who provide individual and/or small group career counseling to students will focus on increasing students' self-awareness for educational and career planning. The use of standardized assessments such as interest inventories can be balanced with the use of informal and nonstandardized assessments such as card sorts, values checklists, and other activities that the counselor and student(s) can work together. The former assessments provide the advantage of being able to be administered to large groups of students simultaneously. Disadvantages include the cost to administer demographically limited normative data and the tendency of students to become more passive participants in the interpretation process. The latter assessments provide the advantage of having low costs associated with them. They also can be more easily adapted to diverse students, and they require active participation by students in the interpretation process. A disadvantage is that they often require more time to administer and interpret than do formal, standardized measures. Thus, the counselor is always confronted with the task of sorting through issues such as financial costs associated with specific interventions and the available time the counselor has to work with students.

Group career counseling interventions offer the opportunity for school counselors to work with more students in less time. They also can be excellent vehicles for delivering information about career development tasks that students either are confronting or will soon confront. Taking a psychoeducational approach to teaching students about career development tasks, and drawing upon the resources of the group to identify strategies for coping with those tasks, is an excellent use of counselor time. Topics that are appropriate for group career counseling include the following: job search strategies, choosing a college, discussing job shadowing experiences, learning about the world of work, and identifying career goals. These topics reflect the student competencies that are identified in the *National Standards for School Counseling Programs* (Campbell & Dahir, 1997) under the career development area.

Given that student–school counselor ratios can climb as high as nearly 1,000:1, it would be naïve at best for school counselors to assume sole responsibility for providing career and educational planning assistance to students. Thus, classroom guidance and career education strategies become crucial to providing career assistance to students. Infusing career concepts into the curriculum has multiple benefits. First, it allows students to connect their academic lives to their lives outside of school. When students understand how school subjects relate to life experience, they often become more motivated and successful learners.

Information related to the student's career planning could be recorded (in hard copy and/or electronically) in an educational and career planning portfolio (Niles & Harris-Bowlsbey, in press). Portfolios offer evolving documentation of each student's career development progress. Portfolios help students and counselors by providing a continual point of reference for focusing career development discussions. They can foster important dialogue among the counselor, student, and student's parents/guardians regarding the student's learning in the career development domain. The school counselor can help the student translate that learning into an educational and career plan. In these ways, portfolios help counselors systematize students' career planning by providing year-by-year information related to the activities (activities in the academic, career, cocurricular, and extracurricular areas) in which a student has engaged, the information the student has learned from those activities, and what activities the student will participate in next to advance in her educational and career planning.

Clearly, school counselors must help their students cope successfully with a wide range of career development tasks. Increasing self-awareness (e.g., values, skills, interests); increasing occupational awareness; developing an accurate understanding of the world of work; learning how to access and use career information resources; understanding how work relates to other salient life roles; coping with parental pressure to select specific occupations; increasing motivation for engaging in career planning; increasing self-efficacy to enhance career decision making; learning job search strategies; understanding how to plan for college, postsecondary employment, or other postsecondary training opportunities; and developing behaviors that are essential for successful employment (being on time, being reliable, working conscientiously, getting along well with others, and anger management) are just some of the career development issues with which school counselors help their students.

UNIVERSITY SETTINGS

College students tend to identify receiving career planning assistance as their area of greatest need (Herr, Cramer, & Niles, 2004; Niles & Harris-Bowlsbey, in press), yet many students do not seem to know what specific on-campus career services are available to them. For example, Fouad et al (2006) found that less than half of the students participating in their study were even aware of career services and even fewer students had used those services. Similar findings exist for students at two-year colleges (Ashburn, 2006). This is a double-edged sword for career practitioners in high education. On the one hand, they must do a better job advertising the services they provide. Most career services offices in higher education offer a full range of career development assistance. On the other hand, the supply of career practitioners in any higher education setting is far less than what would be needed if all, or even most, students were to take full advantage of the services offered. In this way, career counselors in university settings face similar dilemmas to those that school counselors face. They often have substantial demand and limited resources available to meet that demand. In smaller colleges and universities, there may be only a few counselors, at best, who are available to provide career counseling. In larger universities, there may be more counselors, but that number is not likely to keep pace with the larger student population. Thus, providing individual career counseling for an extended period of time is often not possible in university settings. Career practitioners in university settings often focus on brief career counseling interventions. They blend individual counseling with groups, workshops, career planning courses, and computerized career systems. Interventions for first- and second-year university students (and for community college students) often focus on choosing a major, crystallizing career identities, and specifying educational and career plans. Interventions for students in their third and fourth years most often emphasize job search skills and/or developing plans for further education. These interventions can be delivered in workshop as well as one-to-one formats.

Given the time-limited nature of the contact between career counselors and university students, the typical career counseling scenario tends to incorporate standardized assessments (Herr et al., 2004). More recent trends, however, have expanded assessment activities into the subjective, nonstandardized realm (Niles & Harris-Bowlsbey, in press). Using card sorts, values activities, career-laddering techniques, career narratives, and life-career rainbow exercises are all examples of self-assessment activities in the nonstandardized realm. Assessment activities focus on crystallizing self-concepts (Super, 1990; Super et al., 1996) and then connecting to academic majors and occupational options (Crites, 1981). This information provides the focal point for the consolidation, decision-making, and action-planning steps discussed in Chapter 10.

Carson and Dawis (2000) recommend that career counselors in university settings draw upon the work of Gottfredson (1986) to determine which type of assessment instrument might be most appropriate for the student. Specifically, they suggest that career counselors determine whether the student is able to identify occupational options, whether the student's characteristics (values, interests, and abilities) are appropriate for the chosen occupation, whether the student is satisfied with the career choice, and whether the student's plans are realistic. If one or more of these criteria are not met, then the career counselor should seek to understand the underlying problems influencing the student's inability to meet the criteria. Gottfredson (1986) suggests that underlying problems can be differentiated as to whether the student lacks self-knowledge, has life goals and values that are in conflict, has goals and values that conflict with significant people in the student's life, and/or perceives substantial barriers to desired opportunities. Carson and Dawis identify specific career assessment instruments that help students cope with issues related to each of the criteria.

Career planning courses are popular in university settings. They offer the opportunity for counselors to work with larger groups of students. In career planning courses, counselors can address topics such as self-awareness, career awareness, translating self-awareness into educational and occupational plans, job search strategies, understanding the world of work, and learning about career information resources and other important topics central to effective career self-management. Although career planning courses may not eliminate every student's need for career counseling, such courses can offer important information and support to students as they cope with educational and career indecision (Reed, Reardon, Lenz, & Leierer, 2001).

Computer-assisted career guidance systems are also prevalent in university career centers. They offer the advantage of providing students with important self- and occupational information. While students are using the CACGS system, there is little required from the counselor. Thus, CACGS offer the advantage of helping students learn more about themselves and how their characteristics relate to world of work options. The danger in their use is when counselors assume that students can use them without counselor intervention (Niles, 1993). As with secondary school students, when CACGS are used with university students, they should be used in conjunction with counselor assistance, not instead of counselor assistance. Integrating counselor contact before, during (i.e., after the student has had the chance to work with the system but has not yet completed it), and after computer use seems to be an effective strategy for maximizing the benefit that students derive from CACGS.

Career interventions such as the ones described thus far are useful for students experiencing career indecision. They are useful for students who need information about themselves and/or the world of work in order to crystallize career and educational goals. For students who are struggling with career indecisiveness, more career therapy-like interventions are required. Students who are career indecisive often experience concerns that block their career progress. These concerns can include the fear of failure, the fear of success, the fear of experiencing parental disapproval, the fear of making a "wrong" decision, the fear of experiencing peer disapproval, and others. Such concerns require the career counselor to help the student examine the underlying factors associated with the student's fears. Using cognitive behavioral strategies to help students consider the degree to which their assumptions are rational rather than irrational is also an effective career counseling strategy. Whatever concerns the career indecisive student is experiencing, they will need to be addressed before moving on to address the student's career indecision. Obviously, working with career indecisive students requires more counselor time than working with students experiencing career indecision.

Whiston (2000) advises career counselors in university settings to provide career counseling that is interactive and during which the counselor explains the parameters of career counseling to the client at the onset of career counseling. Whiston also suggests that career counselors develop an effective working alliance with their clients and use interventions that challenge and facilitate insight. In essence, Whiston's suggestions are consistent with the suggestions we have provided throughout this book. Active and supportive engagement in career counseling connects with client gains in career development.

COMMUNITY SETTINGS

Private practice settings, assessment centers, mental health centers, substance abuse centers, rehabilitation settings, corrections settings, probation services, military settings, job services offices, one-stop centers, and corporations comprise the majority of settings in which community-based career counseling occurs. The specific process of career counseling will vary dramatically across these settings. So, too, will the career counselor relative to training and credentials. In settings such as private practice, career counselors will most likely be required to be licensed to practice. Private practitioners provide a full range of career counseling assistance to their clients. In other settings, such as corporations, career counselors may have little formal training as counselors and may function more as career coaches addressing their client's needs for career mobility (Niles & Harris-Bowlsbey, 2005). Employment services emphasize connecting job seekers to current job openings. One-stop centers extend the assistance offered by employment services to include connecting clients to other government-related services such as applying for unemployment compensation. The primary purpose of career services across these community-based centers reflects the variety that exists within the career development field. Career interventions can range from a therapy-like experience, career advising, and career coaching to simply providing labor market information.

Because consumers do not always understand that the career counseling process will vary dramatically across community-based settings, counselors must provide clear information on the nature of the service available and the form in which it is provided (counseling, advising, etc.). The same is true of career practitioners. Because their training and credentials will vary dramatically across community-based settings, counselors must provide consumers with a clear description of their training, credentials, and approach to career interventions.

Adults present for career counseling with wide-ranging career concerns. They strive to cope with issues related to tenuous job security, career satisfaction, achieving balance in life roles, coping with occupational stress related to role overload, role ambiguity, difficult supervisors, and hostile relationships with coworkers—to name just a few. It is often the case that, when adults present for career counseling, they also discuss nonwork issues in their sessions (Anderson & Niles, 1995). Thus, career counselors in community settings who work with adult clients experiencing career concerns must be prepared to deal with a variety of work and nonwork concerns. Holistic approaches to career counseling, like those offered by Hansen (2002), Super (1990), and Miller-Tiedeman (1999), are useful resources for providing career interventions that address career development as it is lived—within a holistic framework. More information describing the range of settings in which career practitioners practice can be found in the book entitled *Adult Career Development: Concepts, Issues, and Practices* (Niles, 2003).

SUMMARY

As noted in the beginning of this chapter, the degree to which the career counseling strategies described throughout this book can be applied in any particular setting will likely be determined by the counselor's theoretical orientation, the orientation of the setting in which the counselor works, the research literature related to career counseling practice, the client's needs, and ethical standards.

We encourage career counselors, and those training to become career counselors, to take advantage of the many resources available. The NCDA provides multiple online resources (www.ncda.org) that are directed toward helping career practitioners. *The Career Development Quarterly* is a journal dedicated to helping career practitioners do their work more effectively. Being familiar with the NCDA's career counseling competencies, ethical standards, and ethical standards for using the Internet in career services are important. Professional conferences for career counselors include the NCDA's (usually held in the beginning of the summer) NATCON in Canada (held in January), and conferences of the International Association for Educational and Vocational Guidance (IAEVG), typically held multiple times throughout the year. These conferences provide excellent opportunities to learn more about career counseling and to network with other career practitioners. For prospective counseling students, we recommend considering training programs in which the person teaching the career intervention course is actively engaged in career development theory and practice research and is also personally committed to the career area within counseling.

It has been our goal throughout this book to convey the rich tradition and emerging practices that describe the past and present of career counseling. We believe that effective career counselors are counselors first and that they have also subsequently developed a specialty in career counseling. We realize that the career development process is complex and is composed of intraindividual and contextual variables that influence each person's career trajectory. This complexity makes the career counselor's task a challenging one. Yet, career counselors have the chance to help people cope more effectively with a core life activity. Career counselors can be a source of positive change for individuals and society. They can empower people to live lives that are more satisfying, meaningful, and productive than what they would be without the career counselor's assistance.

The nature of work today presents challenges that workers struggle to cope with successfully. Job security is tenuous at best for many workers. Lifelong learning is a necessity. Balancing work and other life roles feels overwhelming to many. These issues require career counselors to continue their tradition of responding to current career concerns with effective and creative strategies. We hope that the strategies described in this book will help career counselors respond to their clients' career concerns with effective and creative interventions.

Appendix A

THE NATIONAL CAREER DEVELOPMENT ASSOCIATION'S CAREER COUNSELING COMPETENCIES AND PERFORMANCE INDICATORS

http://www.ncda.org Rate yourself according to your competency level for each of the performance indicators listed below. 1 = weak, 2 = average, 3 = strong.

CAREER DEVELOPMENT THEORY

Theory base and knowledge considered essential for professionals engaging in career counseling and development. Demonstration of knowledge of:

1. Counseling theories and associated techniques.

    ___ 1 ___ 2 ___ 3

2. Theories and models of career development.

    ___ 1 ___ 2 ___ 3

3. Individual differences related to gender, sexual orientation, race, ethnicity, and physical and mental capacities.

    ___ 1 ___ 2 ___ 3

4. Theoretical models for career development and associated counseling and information-delivery techniques and resources.

    ___ 1 ___ 2 ___ 3

5. Human growth and development throughout the life span.

    ___ 1 ___ 2 ___ 3

6. Role relationships that facilitate life-work planning.

    ___ 1 ___ 2 ___ 3

7. Information, techniques, and models related to career planning and placement.

    ___ 1 ___ 2 ___ 3

INDIVIDUAL AND GROUP COUNSELING SKILLS

Individual and group counseling competencies considered essential to effective career counseling. Demonstration of ability to:

1. Establish and maintain productive personal relationships with individuals.

   ___ 1   ___ 2   ___ 3

2. Establish and maintain a productive group climate.

   ___ 1   ___ 2   ___ 3

3. Collaborate with clients in identifying personal goals.

   ___ 1   ___ 2   ___ 3

4. Identify and select techniques appropriate to client or group goals and client needs, psychological states, and developmental tasks.

   ___ 1   ___ 2   ___ 3

5. Identify and understand clients' personal characteristics related to career.

   ___ 1   ___ 2   ___ 3

6. Identify and understand familial, subcultural, and cultural structures and functions as they are related to clients' careers.

   ___ 1   ___ 2   ___ 3

7. Identify and understand clients' career decision-making processes.

   ___ 1   ___ 2   ___ 3

8. Identify and understand clients' attitudes toward work and workers.

   ___ 1   ___ 2   ___ 3

9. Identify and understand clients' biases toward work and workers based on gender, race, and cultural stereotypes.

   ___ 1   ___ 2   ___ 3

10. Challenge and encourage clients to take action to prepare for and initiate role transitions by:

    • locating sources of relevant information and experience and

      ___ 1   ___ 2   ___ 3

    • obtaining and interpreting information and experiences, and acquiring skills needed to make role transitions.

      ___ 1   ___ 2   ___ 3

11. Assist the client to acquire a set of employability and job search skills.

___ 1 ___ 2 ___ 3

12. Support and challenge clients to examine life-work roles, including the balance of work, leisure, family, and community in their careers.

___ 1 ___ 2 ___ 3

INDIVIDUAL/GROUP ASSESSMENT

Individual/group assessment skills considered essential for professionals engaging in career counseling. Demonstration of ability to:

1. Assess personal characteristics such as aptitude, achievement, interests, values, and personality traits.

___ 1 ___ 2 ___ 3

2. Assess leisure interests, learning style, life roles, self-concept, career maturity, vocational identity, career indecision, work environment preference (e.g., work satisfaction), and other related life style/development issues.

___ 1 ___ 2 ___ 3

3. Assess conditions of the work environment (such as tasks, expectations, norms, and qualities of the physical and social settings).

___ 1 ___ 2 ___ 3

4. Evaluate and select valid and reliable instruments appropriate to the client's gender, sexual orientation, race, ethnicity, and physical and mental capacities.

___ 1 ___ 2 ___ 3

5. Use computer-delivered assessment measures effectively and appropriately.

___ 1 ___ 2 ___ 3

6. Select assessment techniques appropriate for group administration and those appropriate for individual administration.

___ 1 ___ 2 ___ 3

7. Administer, score, and report findings from career assessment instruments appropriately.

___ 1 ___ 2 ___ 3

8. Interpret data from assessment instruments and present the results to clients and to others.

___ 1 ___ 2 ___ 3

9. Assist the client and others designated by the client to interpret data from assessment instruments.

___ 1 ___ 2 ___ 3

10. Write an accurate report of assessment results.

___ 1 ___ 2 ___ 3

INFORMATION/RESOURCES

Information/resource base and knowledge essential for professionals engaging in career counseling. Demonstration of knowledge of:

1. Education, training, and employment trends; labor market information and resources that provide information about job tasks, functions, salaries, requirements, and future outlooks related to broad occupational fields and individual occupations.

___ 1 ___ 2 ___ 3

2. Resources and skills that clients utilize in life-work planning and management.

___ 1 ___ 2 ___ 3

3. Community/professional resources available to assist clients in career planning, including job search.

___ 1 ___ 2 ___ 3

4. Changing roles of women and men and the implications that this has for education, family, and leisure.

___ 1 ___ 2 ___ 3

5. Methods of good use of computer-based career information delivery systems (CIDS) and computer-assisted career guidance systems (CACGS) to assist with career planning.

___ 1 ___ 2 ___ 3

PROGRAM PROMOTION, MANAGEMENT, AND IMPLEMENTATION

Knowledge and skills necessary to develop, plan, implement, and manage comprehensive career development programs in a variety of settings. Demonstration of knowledge of:

1. Designs that can be used in the organization of career development programs.

___ 1 ___ 2 ___ 3

2. Needs assessment and evaluation techniques and practices.

___ 1 ___ 2 ___ 3

3. Organizational theories, including diagnosis, behavior, planning, organizational communication, and management useful in implementing and administering career development programs.

___ 1 ___ 2 ___ 3

4. Methods of forecasting, budgeting, planning, costing, policy analysis, resource allocation, and quality control.

___ 1 ___ 2 ___ 3

5. Leadership theories and approaches for evaluation and feedback, organizational change, decision-making, and conflict resolution.

___ 1 ___ 2 ___ 3

6. Professional standards and criteria for career development programs.

___ 1 ___ 2 ___ 3

7. Societal trends and state and federal legislation that influence the development and implementation of career development programs.

___ 1 ___ 2 ___ 3

Demonstration of ability to:

8. Implement individual and group programs in career development for specified populations.

___ 1 ___ 2 ___ 3

9. Train others about the appropriate use of computer-based systems for career information and planning.

___ 1 ___ 2 ___ 3

10. Plan, organize, and manage a comprehensive career resource center.

___ 1 ___ 2 ___ 3

11. Implement career development programs in collaboration with others.

___ 1 ___ 2 ___ 3

12. Identify and evaluate staff competencies.

___ 1 ___ 2 ___ 3

13. Mount a marketing and public relations campaign on behalf of career development activities and services.

___ 1 ___ 2 ___ 3

COACHING, CONSULTATION, AND PERFORMANCE IMPROVEMENT

Knowledge and skills considered essential in relating to individuals and organizations that impact the career counseling and development process. Demonstration of ability to:

1. Use consultation theories, strategies, and models.

    __ 1 __ 2 __ 3

2. Establish and maintain a productive consultative relationship with people who can influence a client's career.

    __ 1 __ 2 __ 3

3. Help the general public and legislators to understand the importance of career counseling, career development, and life-work planning.

    __ 1 __ 2 __ 3

4. Impact public policy as it relates to career development and workforce planning.

    __ 1 __ 2 __ 3

5. Analyze future organizational needs and current level of employee skills and develop performance improvement training.

    __ 1 __ 2 __ 3

6. Mentor and coach employees.

    __ 1 __ 2 __ 3

DIVERSE POPULATIONS

Knowledge and skills considered essential in relating to diverse populations that impact career counseling and development processes. Demonstration of ability to:

1. Identify development models and multicultural counseling competencies.

    __ 1 __ 2 __ 3

2. Identify developmental needs unique to various diverse populations, including those of different gender, sexual orientation, ethnic group, race, and physical or mental capacity.

    __ 1 __ 2 __ 3

3. Define career development programs to accommodate needs unique to various diverse populations.

    __ 1 __ 2 __ 3

4. Find appropriate methods or resources to communicate with limited-English-proficient individuals.

___ 1 ___ 2 ___ 3

5. Identify alternative approaches to meet career planning needs for individuals of various diverse populations.

___ 1 ___ 2 ___ 3

6. Identify community resources and establish links to assist clients with specific needs.

___ 1 ___ 2 ___ 3

7. Assist other staff members, professionals, and community members in understanding the unique needs/characteristics of diverse populations with regard to career exploration, employment expectations, and economic/social issues.

___ 1 ___ 2 ___ 3

8. Advocate for the career development and employment of diverse populations.

___ 1 ___ 2 ___ 3

9. Design and deliver career development programs and materials to hard-to-reach populations.

___ 1 ___ 2 ___ 3

SUPERVISION

Knowledge and skills considered essential in critically evaluating counselor or career development facilitator performance and maintaining and improving professional skills. Demonstration of:

1. Ability to recognize own limitations as a career counselor and to seek supervision or refer clients when appropriate.

___ 1 ___ 2 ___ 3

2. Ability to utilize supervision on a regular basis to maintain and improve counselor skills.

___ 1 ___ 2 ___ 3

3. Ability to consult with supervisors and colleagues regarding client and counseling issues and issues related to one's own professional development as a career counselor.

___ 1 ___ 2 ___ 3

4. Knowledge of supervision models and theories.

___1 ___2 ___3

5. Ability to provide effective supervision to career counselors and career development facilitators at different levels of experience.

___1 ___2 ___3

6. Ability to provide effective supervision to career development facilitators at different levels of experience by:

- knowledge of their roles, competencies, and ethical standards,

  ___1 ___2 ___3

- determining their competence in each of the areas included in their certification,

  ___1 ___2 ___3

- further training them in competencies, including interpretation of assessment instruments, and

  ___1 ___2 ___3

- monitoring and mentoring their activities in support of the professional career counselor and scheduling regular consultations for the purpose of reviewing their activities.

  ___1 ___2 ___3

ETHICAL/LEGAL ISSUES

Information base and knowledge essential for the ethical and legal practice of career counseling. Demonstration of knowledge of:

1. Adherence to ethical codes and standards relevant to the profession of career counseling (e.g., NBCC, NCDA, and ACA).

   ___1 ___2 ___3

2. Current ethical and legal issues that affect the practice of career counseling with all populations.

   ___1 ___2 ___3

3. Current ethical/legal issues with regard to the use of computer-assisted career guidance systems.

   ___1 ___2 ___3

4. Ethical standards relating to consultation issues.

   ___1 ___2 ___3

5. State and federal statutes relating to client confidentiality.

___ 1 ___ 2 ___ 3

RESEARCH/EVALUATION

Knowledge and skills considered essential in understanding and conducting research and evaluation in career counseling and development. Demonstration of ability to:

1. Write a research proposal.

___ 1 ___ 2 ___ 3

2. Use types of research and research designs appropriate to career counseling and development research.

___ 1 ___ 2 ___ 3

3. Convey research findings related to the effectiveness of career counseling programs.

___ 1 ___ 2 ___ 3

4. Design, conduct, and use the results of evaluation programs.

___ 1 ___ 2 ___ 3

5. Design evaluation programs that take into account the need of various diverse populations, including persons of both genders, differing sexual orientations, different ethnic and racial backgrounds, and differing physical and mental capacities.

___ 1 ___ 2 ___ 3

6. Apply appropriate statistical procedures to career development research.

___ 1 ___ 2 ___ 3

TECHNOLOGY

Knowledge and skills considered essential in using technology to assist individuals with career planning. Demonstration of knowledge of:

1. Various computer-based guidance and information systems as well as services available on the Internet.

___ 1 ___ 2 ___ 3

2. Standards by which such systems and services are evaluated (e.g., NCDA and ACSCI).

___ 1 ___ 2 ___ 3

3. Ways in which to use computer-based systems and Internet services, to assist individuals with career planning that are consistent with ethical standards.

___ 1 ___ 2 ___ 3

4. Characteristics of clients that make them profit more or less from use of technology-driven systems.

___ 1 ___ 2 ___ 3

5. Methods to evaluate and select a system to meet local needs.

___ 1 ___ 2 ___ 3

Revised by the NCDA Board of Directors, April 1997.

Appendix B

NATIONAL CAREER DEVELOPMENT ASSOCIATION ETHICAL STANDARDS (REVISED 2003)

These Ethical Standards were developed by the National Board for Certified Counselors (NBCC), an independent, voluntary, not-for-profit organization incorporated in 1982. Titled "Code of Ethics" by NBCC and last amended in February 1987, the Ethical Standards were adopted by the National Career Development Association (NCDA) Board of Directors in 1987 and revised in 1991, with minor changes in wording (e.g., the addition of specific references to NCDA members).

Preamble: NCDA is an educational, scientific, and professional organization dedicated to the enhancement of the worth, dignity, potential, and uniqueness of each individual and, thus, to the service of society. This code of ethics enables the NCDA to clarify the nature of ethical responsibilities for present and future professional career counselors.

SECTION A: GENERAL

NCDA members influence the development of the profession by continuous efforts to improve professional practices, services, and research. Professional growth is continuous through the career counselor's career and is exemplified by the development of a philosophy that explains why and how a career counselor functions in the helping relationship. Career counselors must gather data on their effectiveness and be guided by their findings.

1. NCDA members have a responsibility to the clients they are serving and to the institutions within which the services are being performed. Career counselors also strive to assist the respective agency, organization, or institution in providing the highest caliber of professional services. The acceptance of employment in an institution implies that the career counselor is in agreement with the general policies and principles of the institution. Therefore, the professional activities of the career counselor are in accord with the objectives of the institution. If, despite concerted efforts, the career counselor cannot reach agreement with the employer as to acceptable standards of conduct that allow for changes in institutional policy that are conducive to the positive growth and development of clients, then terminating the affiliation should be seriously considered.

2. Ethical behavior among professional associates (e.g., career counselors) must be expected at all times. When accessible information raises doubt as to the ethical behavior of professional colleagues, the NCDA member must make action to attempt to rectify this condition. Such action uses the respective institution's channels first

and then uses procedures established by the American Counseling Association, of which NCDA is a division.

3. NCDA members neither claim nor imply professional qualifications which exceed those possessed, and are responsible for correcting any misrepresentations of these qualifications by others.

4. NCDA members must refuse a private fee or other remuneration for consultation or counseling with persons who are entitled to their services through the career counselor's employing institution or agency. The policies of some agencies may make explicit provisions for staff members to engage in private practice with agency clients. However, should agency clients desire private counseling or consulting services, they must be apprised of other options available to them. Career counselors must not divert to their private practices, legitimate clients in their primary agencies or of the institutions with which they are affiliated.

5. In establishing fees for professional counseling services, NCDA members must consider the financial status of clients and the respective locality. In the event that the established fee status is inappropriate for the client, assistance must be provided in finding comparable services of acceptable cost.

6. NCDA members seek only those positions in the delivery of professional services for which they are professionally qualified.

7. NCDA members recognize their limitations and provide services or only use techniques for which they are qualified by training and/or experience. Career counselors recognize the need, and seek continuing education, to assure competent services.

8. NCDA members are aware of the intimacy in the counseling relationship, maintain respect for the client, and avoid engaging in activities that seek to meet their personal needs at the expense of the client.

9. NCDA members do not condone or engage in sexual harassment which is defined as deliberate or repeated comments, gestures, or physical contacts of a sexual nature.

10. NCDA members avoid bringing their personal or professional issues into the counseling relationship. Through an awareness of the impact of stereotyping and discrimination (e.g., biases based on age, disability, ethnicity, gender, race, religion, or sexual preference), career counselors guard the individual rights and personal dignity of the client in the counseling relationship.

11. NCDA members are accountable at all times for their behavior. They must be aware that all actions and behaviors of a counselor reflect on professional integrity and, when inappropriate, can damage the public trust in the counseling profession. To protect public confidence in the counseling profession, career counselors avoid public behavior that is clearly in violation of accepted moral and legal standards.

12. NCDA members have a social responsibility because their recommendations and professional actions may alter the lives of others. Career counselors remain fully cognizant of their impact and are alert to personal, social, organizational, financial, or political situations or pressures which might lead to misuse of their influence.

13. Products or services provided by NCDA members by means of classroom instruction, public lectures, demonstrations, written articles, radio or television programs, or other types of media must meet the criteria cited in Sections A through F of these Ethical Standards.

SECTION B: COUNSELING RELATIONSHIP

1. The primary obligation of NCDA members is to respect the integrity and promote the welfare of the client, regardless of whether the client is assisted individually or in a group relationship. In a group setting, the career counselor is also responsible for taking reasonable precautions to protect individuals from physical and/or psychological trauma resulting from interaction within the group.

2. The counseling relationship and information resulting from it remains confidential, consistent with the legal obligations of the NCDA member. In a group counseling setting, the career counselor sets a norm of confidentiality regarding all group participants' disclosures.

3. NCDA members know and take into account the traditions and practices of other professional groups with whom they work, and they cooperate fully with such groups. If a person is receiving similar services from another professional, career counselors do not offer their own services directly to such a person. If a career counselor is contacted by a person who is already receiving similar services from another professional, the career counselor carefully considers that professional relationship and proceeds with caution and sensitivity to the therapeutic issues as well as the client's welfare. Career counselors discuss these issues with clients so as to minimize the risk of confusion and conflict.

4. When a client's condition indicates that there is a clear and imminent danger to the client or others, the NCDA member must take reasonable personal action or inform responsible authorities. Consultation with other professionals must be used where possible. The assumption of responsibility for the client's behavior must be taken only after careful deliberation, and the client must be involved in the resumption of responsibility as quickly as possible.

5. Records of the counseling relationship, including interview notes, test data, correspondence, audio or visual tape recordings, electronic data storage, and other documents are to be considered professional information for use in counseling. They should not be considered a part of the records of the institution or agency in which the NCDA member is employed unless specified by state statute or regulation. Revelation to others of counseling material must occur only upon the expressed consent of the client; career counselors must make provisions for maintaining confidentiality in the storage and disposal of records. Career counselors providing information to the public or to subordinates, peers, or supervisors have a responsibility to ensure that the content is general; unidentified client information should be accurate and unbiased, and should consist of objective, factual data.

6. NCDA members must ensure that data maintained in electronic storage are secure. The data must be limited to information that is appropriate and necessary for the services being provided and accessible only to appropriate staff members involved in the provision of services by using the best computer security methods available. Career counselors must also ensure that electronically stored data are destroyed when the information is no longer of value in providing services.

7. Data derived from a counseling relationship for use in counselor training or research shall be confined to content that can be disguised to ensure full protection of the identity of the subject/client and shall be obtained with informed consent.

8. NCDA members must inform clients, before or at the time the counseling relationship commences, of the purposes, goals, techniques, rules and procedures, and limitations that may affect the relationship.

9. All methods of treatment by NCDA members must be clearly indicated to prospective recipients and safety precautions must be taken in their use.

10. NCDA members who have an administrative, supervisory, and/or evaluative relationship with individuals seeking counseling services must not serve as the counselor and should refer the individuals to other professionals. Exceptions are made only in instances where an individual's situation warrants counseling intervention and another alternative is unavailable. Dual relationships with clients that might impair the career counselor's objectivity and professional judgment must be avoided and/or the counseling relationship terminated through referral to another competent professional.

11. When NCDA members determine an inability to be of professional assistance to a potential or existing client, they must, respectively, not initiate the counseling relationship or immediately terminate the relationship. In either event, the career counselor must suggest appropriate alternatives. Career counselors must be knowledgeable about referral resources so that a satisfactory referral can be initiated. In the event that the client declines a suggested referral, the career counselor is not obligated to continue the relationship.

12. NCDA members may choose to consult with any other professionally competent person about a client and must notify clients of this right. Career counselors must avoid placing a consultant in a conflict-of-interest situation that would preclude the consultant's being a proper party to the career counselor's efforts to help the client.

13. NCDA members who counsel clients from cultures different from their own must gain knowledge, personal awareness, and sensitivity pertinent to the client populations served and must incorporate culturally relevant techniques into their practice.

14. When NCDA members engage in intensive counseling with a client, the client's counseling needs should be assessed. When needs exist outside the counselor's expertise, appropriate referrals should be made.

15. NCDA members must screen prospective group counseling participants, especially when the emphasis is on self-understanding and growth through self-disclosure. Career counselors must maintain an awareness of each group participant's welfare throughout the group process.

16. When electronic data and systems are used as a component of counseling services, NCDA members must ensure that the computer application, and any information it contains, is appropriate for the respective needs of clients and is nondiscriminatory. Career counselors must ensure that they themselves have acquired a facilitation level of knowledge with any system they use including hands-on application, search experience, and understanding of the uses of all aspects of the computer-based system. In selecting and/or maintaining computer-based systems that contain career information, career counselors must ensure that the systems provide current, accurate, and locally relevant information. Career counselors must also ensure that clients are intellectually, emotionally, and physically compatible with the use of the computer application and understand its purpose and operation. Client use of a computer application must be evaluated to correct possible problems and assess subsequent needs.

17. NCDA members who develop self-help, stand-alone computer software for use by the general public must first ensure that it is initially designed to function in a stand-alone manner, as opposed to modifying software that was originally designed to require support from a counselor. Secondly, the software must include program statements that provide the user with intended outcomes, suggestions for using the software, descriptions of inappropriately used applications, and descriptions of when and how counseling services might be beneficial. Finally, the manual must include the qualifications of the developer, the development process, validation data, and operating procedures.

SECTION C: MEASUREMENT AND EVALUATION

1. NCDA members must provide specific orientation or information to an examinee prior to and following the administration of assessment instruments or techniques so that the results may be placed in proper perspective with other relevant factors. The purpose of testing and the explicit use of the results must be made known to an examiner prior to testing.

2. In selecting assessment instruments or techniques for use in a given situation or with a particular client, NCDA members must evaluate carefully the instrument's specific theoretical bases and characteristics, validity, reliability, and appropriateness. Career counselors are professionally responsible for using unvalidated information with special care.

3. When making statements to the public about assessment instruments or techniques, NCDA members must provide accurate information and avoid false claims or misconceptions concerning the meaning of psychometrics terms. Special efforts are often required to avoid unwarranted connotations of terms such as IQ and grade-equivalent scores.

4. Because many types of assessment techniques exist, NCDA members must recognize the limits of their competence and perform only those functions for which they have received appropriate training.

5. NCDA members must note when tests are not administered under standard conditions or when unusual behavior or irregularities occur during a testing session and the results must be designated as invalid or of questionable validity. Unsupervised or inadequately supervised assessments, such as mail-in tests, are considered unethical. However, the use of standardized instruments that are designed to be self-administered and self-scored, such as interest inventories, is appropriate.

6. Because prior coaching or dissemination of test materials can invalidate test results, NCDA members are professionally obligated to maintain test security. In addition, conditions that produce most favorable test results must be made known to an examinee (e.g., penalty for guessing).

7. NCDA members must consider psychometrics limitations when selecting and using an instrument, and must be cognizant of the limitations when interpreting the results. When tests are used to classify clients, career counselors must ensure that periodic review and/or re-testing are conducted to prevent client stereotyping.

8. An examinee's welfare, explicit prior understanding, and agreement are the factors used when determining who receives the test results. NCDA members must see

that appropriate interpretation accompanies any release of individual or group test data (e.g., limitations of instrument and norms).

9. NCDA members must ensure that computer-generated assessment administration and scoring programs function properly, thereby providing clients with accurate assessment results.

10. NCDA members who are responsible for making decisions based on assessment results, must have appropriate training and skills in educational and psychological measurement—including validation criteria, test research, and guidelines for test development and use.

11. NCDA members must be cautious when interpreting the results of instruments that possess insufficient technical data, and must explicitly state to examinees the specific purposes for the use of such instruments.

12. NCDA members must proceed with caution when attempting to evaluate and interpret performances of minority group members or other persons who are not represented in the norm group on which the instrument was standardized.

13. NCDA members who develop computer-based interpretations to support the assessment process must ensure that the validity of the interpretations is established prior to the commercial distribution of the computer application.

14. NCDA members recognize that test results may become obsolete, and avoid the misuse of obsolete data.

15. NCDA members must avoid the appropriation, reproduction, or modification of published tests or parts thereof without acknowledgment and permission from the publisher.

SECTION D: RESEARCH AND PUBLICATION

1. NCDA members will adhere to relevant guidelines on research with human subjects. These include:

   a. Code of Federal Regulations, Title 45, Subtitle A, Part 46, as currently issued.
   b. American Psychological Association. (1982). Ethical principles in the conduct of research with human participants. Washington, DC: Author.
   c. American Psychological Association. (1981). Research with human participants. American Psychologist, 36, 633–638.
   d. Family Educational Rights and Privacy Act. (Buckley Amendment to P. L. 93-380 of the Laws of 1974.)
   e. Current federal regulations and various state privacy acts.

2. In planning research activities involving human subjects, NCDA members must be aware of and responsive to all pertinent ethical principles and ensure that the research problem, design, and execution are in full compliance with the principles.

3. The ultimate responsibility for ethical research lies with the principal researcher, although others involved in research activities are ethically obligated and responsible for their own actions.

4. NCDA members who conduct research with human subjects are responsible for the subjects' welfare throughout the experiment and must take all reasonable

precautions to avoid causing injurious psychological, physical, or social effects on their subjects.

5. NCDA members who conduct research must abide by the following basic elements of informed consent:

   a. A fair explanation of the procedures to be followed, including an identification of those which are experimental.

   b. A description of the attendant discomforts and risks.

   c. A description of the benefits to be expected.

   d. A disclosure of appropriate alternative procedures that would be advantageous for subjects.

   e. An offer to answer any inquiries concerning the procedures.

   f. An instruction that subjects are free to withdraw their consent and to discontinue participation in the project or activity at any time.

6. When reporting research results, explicit mention must be made of all the variables and conditions known to the NCDA member that may have affected the outcome of the study or the interpretation of the data.

7. NCDA members who conduct and report research investigations must do so in a manner that minimizes the possibility that the results will be misleading.

8. NCDA members are obligated to make available sufficient original research data to qualified others who may wish to replicate the study.

9. NCDA members who supply data, aid in the research of another person, report research results, or make original data available, must take due care to disguise the identity of respective subjects in the absence of specific authorization from the subject to do otherwise.

10. When conducting and reporting research, NCDA members must be familiar with, and give recognition to, previous work on the topic, must observe all copyright laws, and must follow the principles of giving full credit to those to whom credit is due.

11. NCDA members must give due credit through joint authorship, acknowledgment, footnote statements, or other appropriate means to those who have contributed significantly to the research and/or publication, in accordance with such contributions.

12. NCDA members should communicate to others the results of any research judged to be of professional value. Results that reflect unfavorably on institutions, programs, services, or vested interests must not be withheld.

13. NCDA members who agree to cooperate with another individual in research and/or publication incur an obligation to cooperate as promised in terms of punctuality of performance and with full regard to the completeness and accuracy of the information required.

14. NCDA members must not submit the same manuscript, or one essentially similar in content, for simultaneous publication consideration by two or more journals. In addition, manuscripts that are published in whole or substantial part in another journal or published work should not be submitted for publication without acknowledgment and permission from the previous publication.

SECTION E: CONSULTING

Consultation refers to a voluntary relationship between a professional helper and help-needing individual, group, or social unit in which the consultant is providing help to the client(s) in defining and solving a work-related problem or potential work-related problem with a client or client system.

1. NCDA members acting as consultants must have a high degree of self-awareness of their own values, knowledge, skills, limitations, and needs in entering a helping relationship that involves human and/or organizational change. The focus of the consulting relationship must be on the issues to be resolved and not on the person(s) presenting the problem.

2. In the consulting relationship, the NCDA member and client must understand and agree upon the problem definition, subsequent goals, and predicted consequences of interventions selected.

3. NCDA members must be reasonably certain that they, or the organization represented, have the necessary competencies and resources for giving the kind of help that is needed or that may develop later, and that appropriate referral resources are available to the consultant.

4. NCDA members in a consulting relationship must encourage and cultivate client adaptability and growth toward self-direction. NCDA members must maintain this role consistently and not become a decision maker for clients or create a future dependency on the consultant.

5. NCDA members conscientiously adhere to the NCDA Ethical Standards when announcing consultant availability for services.

SECTION F: PRIVATE PRACTICE

1. NCDA members should assist the profession by facilitating the availability of counseling services in private as well as public settings.

2. In advertising services as private practitioners, NCDA members must advertise in a manner that accurately informs the public of the professional services, expertise, and counseling techniques available.

3. NCDA members who assume an executive leadership role in a private practice organization do not permit their names to be used in professional notices during periods of time when they are not actively engaged in the private practice of counseling.

4. NCDA members may list their highest relevant degree, type, and level of certification and/or license, address, telephone number, office hours, type and/or description of services, and other relevant information. Listed information must not contain false, inaccurate misleading, partial, out-of-context, or otherwise deceptive material or statements.

5. NCDA members who are involved in partnership or corporation with other professionals must, in compliance with the regulations of the locality, clearly specify the separate specialties of each member of the partnership or corporation.

6. NCDA members have an obligation to withdraw from a private-practice counseling relationship if it violates the NCDA Ethical Standards; if the mental or physical condition of the NCDA member renders it difficult to carry out an effective

professional relationship; or if the counseling relationship is no longer productive for the client.

PROCEDURES FOR PROCESSING ETHICAL COMPLAINTS

As a division of the American Counseling Association (ACA) the National Career Development Association (NCDA) adheres to the guidelines and procedures for processing ethical complaints and the disciplinary sanctions adopted by ACA. A complaint against an NCDA member may be filed by any individual or group of individuals ("complainant"), whether or not the complainant is a member of NCDA. Action will not be taken on anonymous complaints.

For specifics on how to file ethical complaints and a description of the guidelines and procedures for processing complaints, contact:

ACA Ethics Committee
c/o Executive Director
American Counseling Association
5999 Stevenson Avenue
Alexandria, VA 22304
(800) 347-6647

Reviewed annually by the NCDA Ethics Committee

NCDA opposes discrimination against any individual on the basis of race, ethnicity, sex, gender identity, sexual orientation, age, religion, socioeconomic status, mental/physical disability, creed, or any other characteristics not specifically relevant to job performance.

(NCDA Board of Directors—January 2003)

Source: The National Career Development Association's *Code of Ethics*, 2003, NCDA. Reprinted with permission of NCDA.

References

Abu Baker, K. (1999). The importance of cultural sensitivity and therapist self-awareness when working with mandatory clients. *Family Process, 38*, 55–67.

ACT, Inc. (1997). *Career planning survey.* Iowa City, IA: Author.

ACT, Inc. (2007). *WorkKeys.* Iowa City, IA: Author.

American Counseling Association. (1999). *Ethical standards for Internet on-line counseling.* Alexandria, VA: Author.

Amundson, N. E. (1989). A model of individual career counseling. *Journal of Employment Counseling, 26*, 132–138.

Amundson, N. E. (1995a). Action planning through the phases of counseling. *Journal of Employment Counseling, 32*, 147–153.

Amundson, N. E. (1995b). An interactive model of career decision making. *Journal of Employment Counseling, 31*, 11–21.

Amundson, N. E. (2003a). *Active engagement: Enhancing the career counselling process* (2nd ed.). Richmond, BC: Ergon Communications.

Amundson, N. E. (2003b). *The physics of living.* Richmond, BC: Ergon Communications.

Amundson, N. E., & Borgen, W. A. (2000). Mandated clients in career or employment counseling. *Journal of Employment Counseling, 37*, 204–215.

Amundson, N. E., & Penner, K. (1998). Parent involved career exploration. *The Career Development Quarterly, 47*, 135–144.

Amundson, N. E., & Poehnell, G. R. (1996). *Career pathways.* Richmond, BC: Ergon Communications.

Amundson, N. E., Westwood, M., & Prefontaine, R. (1995). Cultural bridging and employment counselling with clients from different cultural backgrounds. *Canadian Journal of Counselling, 29*, 206–213.

Anderson, W., & Niles, S. (1995). Career and personal concerns expressed by career counseling clients. *The Career Development Quarterly, 43*, 240–245.

Ashburn, E. (2006). 2-Year college students rarely use advisors. *Chronicle of Higher Education, 53*, A1.

Aubrey, R. F. (1977). Historical development of guidance and counseling and implications for the future. *Personnel and Guidance Journal, 55*, 288–295.

Bennett, G. K., Seashore, H. G., & Wesman, A. G. (1990). *Differential aptitude tests.* San Antonio, TX: Harcourt Assessment.

Bird, B. J. (1989). *Entrepreneurial behavior.* London: Scott Foresman & Company.

Bischoff, M. M., & Tracey, T. J. G. (1995). Client resistance as predicted by therapist behavior: A study of sequential dependence. *Journal of Counseling Psychology, 42*, 487–495.

Bissonnette, D. (1994). *Beyond traditional job development: The art of creating opportunity.* Chatsworth, CA: Milt Wright & Associates.

Bissonnette, D. (2000, January). *Proposal making.* Presentation at the annual NATCON conference, Ottawa, Ontario.

Bloch, D. P. (2005). Complexity, chaos, and nonlinear dynamics: A new perspective on career development theory. *The Career Development Quarterly, 53*, 194–207.

Bohart, A. C., & Tallman, K. (1999). *How clients make therapy work: The process of active self-healing.* Washington, DC: American Psychological Association.

Borgen, W. A., & Amundson, N. E. (1987). The dynamics of unemployment. *Journal of Counseling and Development, 66*, 180–184.

Borgen, W. A., & Amundson, N. E. (1996). *Starting points with youth.* Victoria, BC: Government of British Columbia, MEOST.

Borgen, W. A., & Maglio, A. S. (2007). After services experience of career clients in attempting to implement action plans. *Journal of Employment Counseling, 44*, 173–184.

Bridges, W. (1994). *Job shift.* Reading, MA: Addison-Wesley.

Bright, J. E. H., & Pryor, R. G. L. (2005). The chaos theory of careers: A user's guide. *The Career Development Quarterly, 53*, 291–305.

Brown, D. (1996). Brown's values-based, holistic model of career and life-role choices and satisfaction. In D. Brown, L. Brooks, & Assoc. (Eds.), *Career choice and development* (3rd ed., pp. 337–372). San Francisco: Jossey-Bass.

Brown, D., & Brooks, L. (Eds.). (1990). *Career choice and development: Applying contemporary theories to practice* (2nd ed.). New York: Jossey-Bass.

Burton, M. L., & Wedemeyer, R. A. (1991). *In transition.* New York: HarperBusiness.

Campbell, C., & Dahir, C. (1997). *The national standards for school counseling programs.* Alexandria, VA: American School Counselor Association.

Campbell, D. (1992). *Campbell interest and skill survey.* Minnetonka, MN: National Computer Systems.

Campbell, D., Strong, E. K., & Hansen, J. (1991). *The strong interest inventory.* Palo Alto, CA: Consulting Psychologists Press.

Carroll, M. A. (1997). The multifaceted ethical dimension of treating the mentally ill. *The Hatherleigh guide to ethics in therapy* (pp. 161–179). New York: Hatherleigh Press.

Carson, A. D., & Dawis, R. V. (2000). Determining the appropriateness of career choice assessment. In D. Luzzo (Ed.). *Career counseling of college students: An empirical guide to strategies that work* (pp. 95–120). Washington, DC: American Psychological Association.

Chen, C. P. (2006). Strengthening career human agency. *Journal of Counseling & Development, 84*, 131–138.

Cochran, L. (1997). *Career counseling: A narrative approach.* London: Sage Publication.

Combs, G., & Freedman, J. (1990). *Symbol, story & ceremony.* New York: Norton.

Cooper, R. K. (2001). *The other 90%.* New York: Three Rivers Press.

Corbiere, M., & Amundson, N. E. (2007). Perceptions of the Ways of Mattering by people with mental illness. *The Career Development Quarterly, 56*, 141–149.

Council for the Accreditation of Counseling and Related Educational Programs. (2009). *CACREP standards.* Alexandria, VA: American Counseling Association.

Crites, J. O. (1981). *Career counseling: Models, methods, and materials.* New York: McGraw-Hill.

Crites, J. O., & Savickas, M. (1995). *Career maturity inventory.* Boulder, CO: Crites Career Consultants.

Csikszentmihalyi, M. (1990). *Flow: The psychology of optimal experience.* New York: Harper Perennial.

De Shazer, S. (1985). *Keys to solution in brief therapy.* New York: Norton.

Dixon Rayle, A. (2006). Mattering to others: Implications for the counseling relationship. *Journal of Counseling & Development, 84*, 483–487.

Elliott, G. C., Kao, S., & Grant, A. M. (2004). Mattering: Empirical validation of a social-psychological construct. *Self and Identity, 3*, 339–354.

Fouad, N. A. (1993). Cross-cultural vocational assessment. *The Career Development Quarterly, 42*, 4–13.

Fouad, N., Guilen, A., Harris-Hodge, E., Henry, C., Novakic, A., Terry, S., & Kantameneni, N. (2006). Need, awareness, and use of career services for college students. *Journal of Career Assessment, 14*, 407–420.

Friedman, S. (Ed.). (1993). *The new language of change.* New York: The Guilford Press.

Gati, I. (1986). Making career decisions: A sequential elimination approach. *Journal of Counseling Psychology, 33*, 408–417.

Gelatt, H. B. (1989). Positive uncertainty: A new decision-making framework for counseling. *Journal of Counseling Psychology, 33*, 252–256.

Gottfredson, L. S. (1986). Special groups and the beneficial use of vocational interest inventories. In W. B. Walsh & S. H. Osipow (Eds.), *Advances in vocational psychology: Vol I. The assessment of interests* (pp. 127–198). Hillsdale, NJ: Lawrence Erlbaum.

Gottfredson, L. S. (1996). Gottfredson's theory of circumscription and compromise. In D. Brown & L. Brooks (Eds.), *Career choice and development: Applying contemporary theories to practice* (3rd ed., pp. 179–232). San Francisco: Jossey-Bass.

Gottfredson, L. S., & Holland, J. L. (1996a). *The dictionary of Holland occupational codes.* Odessa, FL: Psychological Assessment Resources.

Gottfredson, L. S., & Holland, J. L. (1996b). *Position classification inventory.* Odessa, FL: Psychological Assessment Resources.

Gysbers, N. C., & Moore, E. J. (1987). *Career counseling skills and techniques for practitioners.* Boston: Allyn & Bacon.

Gysbers, N. C., Heppner, M. J., & Johnston, J. A. (2003). *Career counseling: Process, issues, and techniques* (2nd ed.). Boston: Allyn & Bacon.

Hampden-Turner, C., & Trompenaars, F. (2000). *Building cross-cultural competence.* New York: John Wiley & Sons.

Hansen, L. S. (2002). Integrative life planning: A holistic theory for career counseling with adults. In S. Niles (Ed.), *Adult career development: Concepts, issues, and practices* (3rd ed., pp. 57–75). Tulsa, OK: National Career Development Association.

Harrington, T., & O'shea, A. (2000). *Harrington–O'shea career decision making system.* Circle Pines, MN: American Guidance Service.

Harrington, T. F., & Harrigan, T. A. (2006). Practice and research in career counseling and Development. *The Career Development Quarterly, 55,* 98–167.

Harris-Bowlsbey, J., Riley Dikel, M., & Sampson, J. P., Jr. (2002). *The Internet: A tool for career planning* (2nd ed.). Tulsa, OK: National Career Development Association.

Herr, E. L. (1989). Career development and mental health. *Journal of Career Development, 16,* 5–18.

Herr, E. L. (1999). *Counseling in a dynamic society: Contexts & practices for the 21st century.* Alexandria, VA: American Counseling Association.

Herr, E. L. (2001). Career development and its practice: A historical perspective. *The Career Development Quarterly, 49,* 196–211.

Herr, E. L., Cramer, S. H., & Niles, S. G. (2004). *Career guidance and counseling through the lifespan: Systemic approaches.* New York: HarperCollins.

Hofstede, G. (1997). *Cultures and organizations.* New York: McGraw-Hill.

Holland, J. L. (1985). *Vocational preference inventory.* Odessa, FL: Psychological Assessment Resources.

Holland, J. L. (1994a). *The occupations finder.* Odessa, FL: Psychological Assessment Resources.

Holland, J. L. (1994b). *Self-directed search.* Odessa, FL: Psychological Assessment Resources.

Holland, J. L. (1997). *Making vocational choices: A theory of vocational personalities and work environments* (3rd ed.). Odessa, FL: Psychological Assessment Resources.

Holmberg, K., Rosen, D., & Holland, J. L. (1999). *The leisure activities finder.* Odessa, FL: Psychological Assessment Resources.

Inkson, K. (2007). *Understanding careers: The metaphors of working lives.* Thousand Oaks: Sage Publications.

Inkson, K., & Amundson, N. (2002). Career metaphors and their application in theory and counseling practice. *Journal of Employment Counseling, 39,* 98–108.

Jackson, D. N. (1991). *Jackson vocational interest survey.* Port Huron, MI: Sigma Assessment Systems.

Johansen, C. B. (1984). *Career assessment inventory.* Minneapolis, MN: National Computer Systems, Inc.

Kelly, E. W. (1997). Relationship-centered counseling: A humanistic model of integration. *Journal of Counseling and Development, 75,* 337–345.

Kelly, G. A. (1955). *A theory of personality: The psychology of personal constructs.* New York: Norton.

Klausmeier, H. J., & Goodwin, W. (1966). Learning and human abilities. In *Educational psychology* (2nd ed.). New York: Harper & Row.

Knapp, R. R., & Knapp, L. (1992). *Career occupational preference survey.* San Diego, CA: EDITS.

Kroese, J. M., Hynd, G. W., Knight, D. F., Hiemenz, J. R., & Hallo, J. (2000). Clinical appraisal of spelling ability and its relationship to phonemic awareness (blending, segmenting, elision, and reversal), phonological memory, and reading in reading disabled, ADHD, and normal children. *Reading and Writing: An Interdisciplinary Journal, 13,* 105–131.

Krumboltz, J. D. (1991). *The career beliefs inventory.* Palo Alto, CA: Consulting Psychologists Press.

Krumboltz, J. D. (1996). A learning theory of career counseling. In M. Savickas & B. Walsh (Eds.), *Integrating career theory and practice* (pp. 233–280). Palo Alto, CA: Consulting Psychologists Books.

Krumboltz, J. D., & Baker, R. (1973). Behavioral counseling for vocational decisions. In H. Borow (Ed.), *Career guidance for a new age* (pp. 235–284). Boston: Houghton Mifflin.

Kuder, F., & Zytowski, D. (2007). *Kuder career search with person match.* Adel, IA: Kuder, Inc.

Kuder, Inc. (2006). *Kuder skills assessment.* Adel, IA: Author.

Lapan, R. T. *Career development across the K-16 years.* (2004). Alexandria, VA: American Counseling Association.

Leong, F. (1996). Toward an integrative model for cross-cultural counseling and psychotherapy. *Applied and preventative psychology, 5,* 189–209.

Levey, J., & Levey, M. (1998). *Living in balance: A dynamic approach for creating harmony and wholeness in a chaotic world.* New York: MJF Books.

Maher, A. R., Murphy, R. G., Gagnon, R., & Gingras, N. (1994). The counsellor as a cause and cure of client resistance. *Canadian Journal of Counselling, 28,* 125–134.

Maslow, A. H. (1954). *Motivation and personality.* New York: Harper & Row.

McCormick, R., & Amundson, N. (1997). A career-life planning model for First Nations people. *Journal of Employment Counseling, 34,* 171–179.

McMahon, M. (2005). Career counseling: Applying the systems theory framework of career development. *Journal of Employment Counseling, 42,* 29–38.

Miller, W. R., & Rollnick, S. (2002). *Motivational interviewing: Preparing people for change* (2nd ed.). New York: Guilford Press.

Miller-Tiedeman, A. (1999). *Learning, practicing, and living the new careering.* Philadelphia, PA: Accelerated Development.

Muscat, A. C. (2005). Ready, set, go: The transtheoretical model of change and motivational interviewing for "fringe" clients. *Journal of Employment Counseling, 42,* 179–191.

Myers, I., & Briggs, K. (1993). *The Myers–Briggs type indicator.* Palo Alto, CA: Consulting Psychologists Press.

National Board of Certified Counselors. (2007). *The practice of Internet counseling .* Greensboro, NC: Author.

National Career Development Association. (1997). *NCDA guidelines for the use of the Internet for provision of career information and planning services.* Columbus, OH: Author.

Newman, C. F. (1994). Understanding client resistance: Methods for enhancing motivation to change. *Cognitive and behavioral practice, 1,* 47–69.

Niles, S. G. (1993). The timing of counselor contact in the use of a computer information delivery system with adult career counseling clients. *Journal of Employment Counseling, 30,* 2–12.

Niles, S. G. (Ed.). (2003). Adult career development: Concepts, issues and practices (3rd ed.). Tulsa, OK: National Career Development Association.

Niles, S. G., Anderson, W. P., Jr., & Cover, S. (2000). Comparing intake concerns and goals with career counseling concerns. *The Career Development Quarterly, 49,* 135–145.

Niles, S. G., & Harris-Bowlsbey, J. (in press). *Career development interventions in the 21st century.* (3rd ed.). Upper Saddle River, NJ: Merrill/Prentice Hall.

O'Hanlon, W. H., & Weiner-Davis, M. (1989). *In search of solutions: A new direction in psychotherapy.* New York: Norton.

Osipow, S. H., Carney, C. G., Winer, J., Yanico, B., & Koschier, M. (1997). *Career decision scale.* Odessa, FL: Psychological Assessment Resources.

Parsons, F. (1909). *Choosing a vocation.* Boston: Houghton Mifflin.

Patsula, P. (1992). *The assessment component of employment counselling*. Ottawa: Human Resources Development Canada.

Pryor, R. G. L., Amundson, N. E., & Bright, J. E. H. (in press). Probabilities and possibilities: The strategic counseling implications of the chaos theory of careers. *Career Development Quarterly*.

Pryor, R. G. L., & Bright, J. E. H. (2006). Counseling chaos: Techniques for practitioners. *Journal of Employment Counseling, 43*, 2–17.

Reed, C. A., Reardon, R. C., Lenz, J. G., & Leierer, S. J. (2001). A cognitive career course: From theory to practice. *The Career Development Quarterly, 50*, 158–167.

Richardson, M. S. (1996). From career counseling to counseling/psychotherapy and work, jobs, and career. In M. L. Savickas & W. B. Walsh (Eds.), *Handbook of career counseling theory and practice* (pp. 347–360). Palo Alto, CA: Davies-Black Publishing.

Rifkin, J. (1995). *The end of work*. New York: Putnam.

Roe, A. (1956). *The psychology of occupations*. New York: Wiley.

Rogers, C. R. (1951). *Client-centered therapy*. Boston: Houghton Mifflin.

Rogers, C. R. (1961). *On becoming a person*. Boston: Houghton Mifflin.

Rogers, C. R. (1989). A client-centered/person-centered approach to therapy. In H. Kirschenbaum & V. L. Henderson (Eds.), *The Carl Rogers reader* (pp. 135–152). Boston: Houghton Mifflin (Original work published 1986).

Rosen, D., Holmberg, K., & Holland, J. L. (1999). *The educational opportunities finder*. Odessa, FL: Psychological Assessment Resources.

Sampson, J. P., Jr., Carr, D. L., Panke, J., Arkin, S., Minville, M., & Vernick, S. H. (2001). Design strategies for need-based Internet Web sites in counseling (technical report no. 28). Tallahassee, FL: Florida State University, Center for the Study of Technology in Counseling and Career Development (Online).

Sampson, J. P., Jr., Peterson, G. W., Lenz, J. G., Reardon, R. C., & Saunders, D. E. (1996). *Career thoughts inventory*. Odessa, FL: Psychological Assessment Resources.

Savickas, M. L. (1993). Career in the post-modern era. *Journal of Cognitive Psychotherapy: An International Quarterly, 7*, 205–215.

Savickas, M. L. (2000). Renovating the psychology of careers for the 21st century. In A. Collin & R. Young (Eds.), *The future of career* (pp. 53–68). Cambridge, England: Cambridge University Press.

Savickas, M. L. (2005). The theory and practice of career construction. In S. D. Brown & R. W. Lent (Eds.). *Career development and counseling: Putting theory and research to work* (pp. 42–70). Hoboken, NJ: John Wiley & Sons.

Schlossberg, N. K., Lynch, A. Q., & Chickering, A. W. (1989). *Improving higher education environments for adults*. San Francisco, CA: Jossey-Bass.

Stahl, S. A., Hare, V. C., Sinatra, R., & Gregory, J. F. (1991). Defining the role of prior knowledge and vocabulary in reading comprehension: The retiring of number 41. *Journal of Reading Behavior, 23*, 487–507.

Storey, J. (2000). "Fracture lines" in the career environment. In A. Collins & R. Young (Eds.), *The future of career* (pp. 21–36). Cambridge: Cambridge University Press.

Super, D. E. (1963). Self-Concepts in Vocational Development. In D. E. Super, R. Starishevsky, N. Matlin, & J. P. Jordaan (Eds.). *Career development: Self-concept theory* (pp. 17–32). New York: College Entrance Examination Board.

Super, D. E. (Ed.). (1970). *Computer-assisted counseling*. New York: Teachers College, Columbia University.

Super, D. E. (1980). A life-span, life-space approach to career development. *Journal of Vocational Behavior, 16*, 282–298.

Super, D. E. (1990). Career and life development. In D. Brown & L. Brooks (Eds.), *Career choice and development: Applying contemporary theories to practice* (2nd ed., pp. 197–261). San Francisco: Jossey-Bass.

Super, D. E., Savickas, M. L., & Super, C. M. (1996). The life-span, life-space approach to careers. In D. Brown & L. Brooks (Eds.), *Career choice and development: Applying contemporary theories to practice* (3rd ed., pp. 121–178). San Francisco: Jossey-Bass.

Super, D. E., Thompson, A. S., Lindeman, R. H., Jordaan, J. P., & Myers, R. A. (1984). *Career development inventory*. Palo Alto, CA: Consulting Psychologists Press.

Taber, B. J., & Luzzo, D. A. (1999). *ACT Research Report 99-3: A comprehensive review of research evaluating the effectiveness of DISCOVER in promoting career development*. Iowa City, IA: ACT, Inc.

Tretheway, A. (1997). Resistance, identity and empowerment: A post modern feminist analysis of clients in a human service organization. *Communication Monographs, 64*, 281–301.

Trevor-Roberts, E. (2006). Are you sure? The role of uncertainty in career. *Journal of Employment Counseling, 43*, 98–116.

Tursi, M. M., & Cochran, J. L. (2006). Cognitive-behavioral tasks accomplished in a person-centered relational framework. *Journal of Counseling & Development, 84*, 387–398.

United States Department of Labor (1999). *O*Net Abilities Profiler*. Washington, DC: Author.

United States Department of Labor (2007). *O*Net Occupational Database*. Washington, DC Author.

United States Employment Service. (1982). *The general aptitude test battery*. Washington, DC: Author.

United States Employment Service. (2002). *O*Net Interest Profiler*. Washington, DC: Author.

Walter, J. L., & Peller, J. E. (1992). *Becoming solution-focused in brief therapy*. New York: Brunner/Mazel.

Weinrach, S. G., & Thomas, K. R. (1996). The counseling profession's commitment to diversity-sensitive counseling: A critical reassessment. *Journal of Counseling and Development, 73*, 472–477.

Westwood, M., Amundson, N., & Borgen, W. (1994). *Starting points: Finding your route to employment*. Ottawa: Human Resources Development Canada.

Whiston, S. (2000). Individual career counseling. In D. Luzzo (Ed.), *Career counseling of college students: An empirical guide to strategies that work* (pp. 137–156). Washington, DC: American Psychological Association.

Zytowski, D. G., & Kuder, F. (2007). *Kuder career search with person match*. Adel, IA: Kuder, Inc.

Index